The Best of

Simple!
(i t s)

Easy Recipes for Today's
Tastes and Lifestyles

by ann heller

• *DEDICATION*

This is for all the readers who said their clippings were tattered and yellowed with age: A book of the best, plus a pocket to save future favorites.

Published by the *Dayton Daily News*
45 S. Ludlow Street • Dayton, Ohio 45402

ISBN: 0-9616347-6-6

••• *PANTRY* •••

Most people have a poorly stocked selection of aging spices, herbs and ethnic condiments and flavorings on the shelves. Take the time to go to the store and invest in a small flavor pantry. Think of these as essentials for good cooking. You'll need them for some of the recipes in this book. And remember that a good cook always keeps fresh garlic, lemons and a chunk of Parmesan cheese on hand.

• *HERBS AND SPICES*

Bay leaves, cayenne pepper, chili powder, cinnamon, cloves, coriander, cumin, curry powder, kosher or sea salt, whole nutmeg, Old Bay Seasoning, oregano, red pepper flakes and dried red chilies, tarragon, thyme.

• *SEASONINGS*

Canned jalapeno peppers, Oriental chili-garlic sauce, Dijon mustard, hot pepper sauce, maple syrup, Oriental sesame oil, olive oil, red wine vinegar, rice wine vinegar, soy sauce, dry vermouth for cooking, and Worcestershire sauce.

• *STAPLES*

Reduced-salt chicken broth, unsweetened coconut milk, dried mushrooms, nuts (macadamia, peanuts, pecans, almonds, black walnuts, pine nuts), imported black olives, pasta, basmati and jasmine rice and wild rice.

• • • • • • • • •

- *NOTES*

• APPETIZERS

• *BOURBON PECANS*

Anyone can open a jar of olives and a can of nuts and set them out for a party. But that's so boring; it tells your guests you don't think much of them.

By getting a head start, you can can offer such temptations as bourbon spiced nuts and marinated olives.

Nuts go fast at any party—people tend to down them by the handful rather than nibble on them—so fix plenty.

These bourbon pecans have a little sweetness and more than a smidgen of heat. They're perfect for a holiday of this season.

Makes 4 cups

3 ounces bourbon
1/2 cup sugar
1/2 teaspoon Angostura
   bitters, optional
1 tablespoon Worcestershire sauce
1 tablespoon corn oil

1 pound pecan halves
1/2 teaspoon cayenne pepper
1/2 teaspoon salt
1/4 teaspoon black pepper
1 teaspoon ground cumin

Preheat oven to 325 degrees.

Simmer the bourbon to reduce it to 3 tablespoons. Combine the reduced bourbon, sugar, bitters, Worcestershire sauce and corn oil.

Blanch the pecans for 1 minute in boiling water, then drain the nuts. Turn the hot nuts into a bowl and toss with the bourbon mixture. Let stand 10 minutes, then spread on a foil-lined, rimmed cookie sheet, pouring the remaining bourbon marinade over them.

Bake for 30 to 35 minutes, stirring every 10 minutes. When nuts are crisp and lightly brown, and the liquid has evaporated, turn the nuts into a bowl.

Combine the cayenne, salt, pepper and cumin. Sprinkle over the nuts while tossing them.

Turn out onto a clean, foil-lined cookie sheet to dry in a single layer. Store in an airtight container.

• GRILLED PIZZA

Innovative restaurant chefs have been offering grilled pizza for a while but now backyard grill cooks can capture the flavor at home by turning a kettle grill into a makeshift oven.

What you get is a crispy crust, a smoky flavor and the guarantee of a hot pizza that beats anything delivered to your door.

Just start with one of those prebaked crusts such as Boboli and have your favorite toppings ready. The only other essential is a handful of smoking chips.

Makes 4 servings

4 individual-sized Boboli or other
  partly precooked pizza shell
4 tablespoons olive oil
1 large tomato, thinly sliced
salt

1/2 teaspoon minced fresh garlic
1/2 cup chopped fresh herbs*
1/2 cup grated fontina cheese
2 tablespoons Parmesan cheese

Place a handful or two of wood smoking chips in water to cover and soak for at least half an hour.

Open all vents on the grill. Place a brick in the center of a kettle grill and place hardwood charcoal briquettes on one side of the brick and light them.

When briquettes are lightly covered with ash (20 to 25 minutes) spread only on one side of the grill. A medium-hot fire is ideal; you do not want any flames visible.

Brush each pizza shell with some of the oil. Cut tomato slices into fourths. Place at least four pieces of tomato on each pizza and sprinkle with salt, the garlic and herbs. Sprinkle cheeses over the pizzas and drizzle each with olive oil.

Just before cooking the pizza, drain the smoking chips and scatter on the edges of the hot coals. Place the pizza on the cooking grate, to the side. Do NOT place directly over the coals. Put the cover on the grill with the vents open and cook for 7 to 15 minutes, depending on the heat of your fire. (Start checking at 7 minutes; you may need to rearrange the pizzas to prevent scorching on the side close to the fire.)

When the cheese is melted, remove and cut into wedges.

*Herbs darken with heat; to add fresh color, reserve a tablespoon and sprinkle over the hot pizzas as you take them off the grill.

• BRUSCHETTA

Bruschetta is real Italian garlic bread.

Unlike the American bastardization, which is slathered in butter, overpowered with garlic powder and ersatz Parmesan cheese, wrapped in foil and virtually steamed, the Italian original is a masterpiece of simplicity.

Essentially, it is just good bread toasted over a charcoal or wood fire, rubbed with fresh garlic and generously anointed with fragrant oil.

That's fine as an appetizer or snack, but add a slice of tomato or a mound of chopped tomato and a little basil and it becomes a pleasant lunch. Another variation is to top the bread with leaves of arugula, the peppery Italian herb sometimes served as a salad.

Makes 2 to 4 servings

4 thick slices country bread*	coarse salt
1 large clove garlic	freshly ground black pepper
4 tablespoons extra virgin olive oil	8 small leaves basil
1 large tomato, peeled	

Toast the bread over a charcoal fire until golden. While the bread is still hot, rub with the cut side of a clove of garlic. Arrange on a platter and drizzle with the oil. (The bruschetta can be served as is, or continue with the recipe).

Cut the tomato in half and squeeze lightly to remove any excess seeds. Cut into four slices and arrange on the bread. Sprinkle with coarse salt and freshly ground pepper. Tear the basil leaves and sprinkle on top. Serve immediately.

*You need a sturdy, crusty bread. Ciabiatta, an Italian-style loaf, is worth looking for.

• PESTO CHEESE TORTA

This recipe for a pretty green and white pesto cheese torta, is a staple in my Christmas repertoire. I guarantee this ultra-rich appetizer will be a hit, especially if you have some of your own homemade pesto sauce in the freezer. (You shouldn't go through the summer without making some for a long, cold winter without fresh basil.) If not, you can use the canned pesto sauce available at gourmet food stores, but you'll need at least 3/4 cup.

Like most of my favorite appetizers, it can be made ahead.

Makes 10 servings

1 3-ounce and 1 8-ounce package cream cheese
2/3 pound unsalted butter
1 batch (3/4 to 1 cup) pesto (see index)

Let cream cheese and butter sit at room temperature until soft. Beat with an electric mixer until blended and smooth.

Use dampened cheesecloth to line a 4-cup mold, such as a loaf pan, charlotte mold, even a clean flowerpot. Use your fingers to make a layer with 1/6 of the cheese, then add 1/6 of the pesto, extending it to the sides of the mold so that it will show when unmolded. Continue making layers, finishing with the cheese.

Fold ends of cheesecloth over torta and press down lightly with your hands to compact. Chill until firm when pressed, about 1 1/2 hours. Invert on a serving dish and pull off cheesecloth. (If you don't, it will act as a wick and cause green color to blend into cheese.) Refrigerate the torta until serving time.

Garnish with toasted pine nuts and, if you can find it, a sprig of basil, which is available in small packages at some supermarkets. Serve with plain crackers.

Well wrapped and refrigerated, the torta will keep five days.

• CRUSTY BAKED CHEESE

The Danes were always a hit at food editors conferences that used to be held in Chicago. The people who came to promote their cuisine were lively and the food was always wonderful.

One year the hit was an appetizer of Danish cheese baked in puff pastry with herbs. I introduced the easy appetizer back in Dayton and it caught on widely. It can be assembled ahead of time in minutes, then just popped in the oven an hour before serving. You can spend that time putting final touches on a party.

Makes 8 servings

1 7-ounce round creamy havarti or Camembert cheese
1 tablespoon Dijon mustard
1/4 cup fresh herbs *
1 sheet frozen puff pastry
1 egg, lightly beaten

Thaw the puff pastry in the refrigerator. Spread the top of the cheese round with mustard, then cover with the herbs, pressing into the mustard. Remove one pastry sheet from the package and unfold.

Using a 9-inch pie plate as a pattern, cut a circle in the pastry, reserving scraps. Center cheese on the pastry, herb side down. Gather edges of pastry over cheese, moistening overlapping edges and pinching tightly. Place on greased foil on a shallow baking sheet, seam-side down. Brush all over with beaten egg.

Roll scraps and cut decorative designs; arrange on top. Chill for at least 30 minutes. Brush again with egg.

Cup foil around the side of cheese (so that it keeps its shape) and bake in a preheated 375-degree oven for 15 minutes. Pull foil away from sides and brush again with egg. Bake 15 minutes more until golden brown.

Cool for 30 minutes before serving. Cut into wedges.

*Use fresh parsley, chives, dill, basil and watercress. Dried dill can be substituted for fresh.

GARLIC BLUE CHEESE SPREAD

Nancy Radke is an American in love with Italian food and her newsletter, "Ciao," shares the passion.

A few years ago she visited Dayton and one of the things she fixed was a gutsy Italian cheese spread, laced with garlic and blue cheese and topped with toasted walnuts.

It should be made a day or two ahead, which makes it easy to serve at parties.

Don't let the amount of garlic deter you; blanching the cloves tames the taste.

Makes 1 1/2 cups

1 medium head of garlic,
   separated into unpeeled cloves
4 ounces blue cheese
4 ounces whole milk ricotta cheese
4 ounces cream cheese

1/2 teaspoon salt
1 tablespoon chopped fresh sage*
1 tablespoon toasted
   walnuts, finely chopped

Cook garlic in boiling water for 15 to 20 minutes, until tender. Drain and squeeze garlic out of peel. Crush garlic with the side of a knife and measure out 2 tablespoons.

Crumble blue cheese into the bowl of a food processor; add other cheeses, garlic and process for 5 seconds. Add salt and sage and process for 5 seconds.

Pack in a serving bowl, cover and refrigerate at least 24 hours. Before serving top with chopped nuts. Serve with pita crisps, preferably homemade.

* Fresh sage is available in small packets at major groceries.

• TIP

To make your own pita chips split 6-inch pita breads open and brush with oil. Cut each pita half into six wedges. Sprinkle with salt and herbs, if desired. Arrange in a single layer on baking sheets and bake for 5 to 10 minutes in a preheated 400-degree oven until crisp and golden.

• SMOKED FISH PATE

Promoters of under-utilized "trash" fish, as they call them, served samples to food editors at a Washington conference one year. Most didn't make the hit parade of seafood, but an appetizer of smoked fish pate was scooped up and relished. More a spread than a pate, it was mounded on a platter with an array of smoked fish, apples and grapes.

Later on, we found out how simple it is to prepare.

It's made with smoked bluefish, which is hard to find around here, but any inexpensive smoked fish can be used. This is not the place to use fine cold-smoked salmon.

This appetizer can be made ahead, but be sure to bring it back to room temperature before serving. Fluff the mixture with a fork. Serve with crackers, slices of good French bread and fruit.

Makes 6 appetizer servings

1/4 pound smoked bluefish or other smoked fish
1/4 pound unsalted butter at room temperature
3 ounces cream cheese
1 teaspoon prepared horseradish

Remove and discard the skin from the fish and crumble the fish into a food processor or mixing bowl. Add the softened butter and cream cheese. Process or beat with an electric mixer until thoroughly combined and fluffy. Season with the horseradish, adding more to add an extra zip.

Optional additions include 1/4 teaspoon Worcestershire sauce, a squirt of lemon juice and a teaspoon of chopped onion.

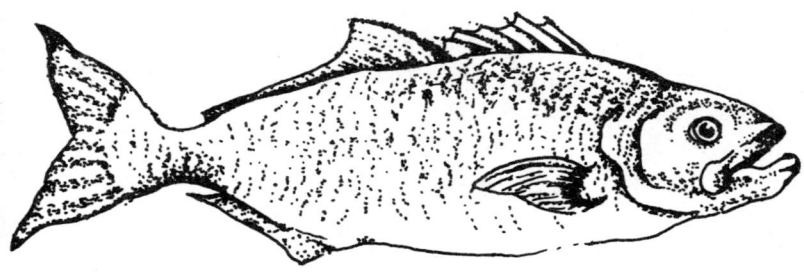

• SCALLOP SEVICHE

When the temperature tops 90, who can cook? Even in an air-conditioned house, the idea of hot food is oppressive.

You won't catch me near the grill, or heating up my house, until the temperature drops a lot.

But man or woman can't live by raw fruits and vegetables alone, so this is the time for another kind of cooking.

Our neighbors to the south make seviche, the marinated seafood cocktail in which a marinade of lime juice cooks the fish. This is my favorite of the many recipes I've tried.

It uses an abundant amount of cilantro, the parsley look-alike that packs a punch. It's usually available at major supermarkets.

Makes 6 servings

1 ½ pounds fresh sea scallops
1 ½ cups fresh lime juice
3 cloves garlic, minced
1 ½ red bell peppers,
   cut into thin strips
2 mild green chilies,
   fresh or canned*

3/4 bunch fresh cilantro, chopped
2 tomatoes, cored, peeled,
   seeded and chopped
2 jalapeno chilies,
   finely chopped
3/4 cup olive oil

If the scallops are very large, cut them in halves or quarters. Place the scallops in a glass or stainless steel bowl; add the lime juice, covering the scallops entirely. Marinate at least 1 hour; 4 or 5 hours will give the scallops a more cooked appearance.

Shortly before serving, add the remaining ingredients and mix well. Serve using a slotted spoon. For added flair, spoon into large wine goblets.

* If using canned chiles, rinse them well to remove the taste of the brine.

• CHICKEN SATAY

Satays are street food found widely in countries such as Singapore, Malaysia and Indonesia. For Americans, they have become split-second appetizers.

Morsels of chicken or beef are skewered and marinated ahead of time. They can be refrigerated until needed, then cooked for under 5 minutes on a grill.

The dipping sauce, a Thai-style peanut sauce, can also be made ahead.

Makes 4 servings

    4 chicken breast halves, skinned and boned
    1/2 cup unsweetened coconut milk*
    1/2 teaspoon turmeric
    1/4 teaspoon curry powder
    1/8 teaspoon salt
    peanut sauce (see index)

Slice the chicken lengthwise, holding the knife at a slant, cutting into 1/4-inch thick slices about an inch wide. Mix the coconut milk, turmeric, curry and salt in a mixing bowl.

Thread the chicken on bamboo skewers that have been soaked in water. The chicken should lie flat on the skewers.

Marinate in the coconut milk mixture for at least 1 hour. (The chicken can be refrigerated and marinated overnight if desired.)

Grill over hot coals or broil. On a hot fire, the satays will cook in a minute or two per side.

Serve with peanut sauce and cucumber salad. (see index.)

*Do not use coconut cream meant for drinks. Coconut milk is available at Oriental markets.

NOTE: These will be thin bites of chicken. If you want a more substantial-looking appetizer, slice the breasts lengthwise, then cut into 1-inch cubes. Cook these several minutes longer.

• SOUPS

• AFRICAN NUT SOUP

I've had enough bad peanut soups so I didn't order it when The Winds restaurant in Yellow Springs put it on the menu, under the name African groundnut soup. Fortunately, someone at my table did.

This soup, created by owner by M.K. Smith, is in a league by itself. Despite the name, it has accents of the Orient.

It's a rich soup that should be served as a first course.

Makes 6 servings

2 tablespoons butter
1 tablespoon sesame oil
1 to 2 cloves garlic, minced
2 tablespoons minced fresh
　ginger root
1 bunch green onions, chopped
3 cups mushrooms, quartered
1 tablespoon flour

3 cups hot vegetable or
　chicken broth
8 ounces unsalted crunchy
　peanut butter*
2 cups half and half
2 tablespoons soy sauce
1/4 teaspoon ground black pepper

In a 2-quart saucepan, heat the butter and sesame oil over a low flame. Add the garlic, ginger root, green onion and cook, stirring over low heat for 3 minutes. Be careful not to burn the garlic.

Add the mushrooms. Saute for 5 minutes more, stirring occasionally. Sprinkle the flour over. Stir, scraping the bottom of the pan, for 3 or 4 minutes. Whisk in the simmering stock.

Place the peanut butter in a bowl and whisk in the heated half and half, first making a paste and adding the liquid gradually. Pour the mixture into the saucepan of soup. Stir well and season with soy sauce and fresh ground pepper.

If using canned chicken stock, taste the soup before seasoning with soy sauce as tinned broth may be very salty. If using salted peanut butter, reduce soy sauce seasoning.

NOTE: Heating the half and half makes it easier to incorporate with the peanut butter.

*Look for unsalted peanut butter at nut specialty stores and some supermarket delis.

• BLUE SATIN SOUP

Maytag Dairy Farms, that Iowa mail-order cheese farm, seduced me when it sent a cheese sample and tucked in some wonderful blue cheese. It's the darling of the new breed of American chefs who have made a religion of using American-made and grown ingredients.

And Maytag added a few new recipes, including this one for Blue Satin Soup. It is as sensuous as satin.

Makes 4 cups

4 tablespoons butter
1/4 cup each very finely minced
   green onion, green pepper
   and celery
1/2 cup flour
1 14-ounce can chicken
   broth, heated

4 ounces blue cheese crumbled
1 cup coffee cream
1 cup whole milk
2 ounces dry sherry or Marsala
1/4 teaspoon freshly
   ground pepper

In a heavy saucepan, melt butter and saute the minced vegetables over very low heat until soft but not browned. Stir occasionally.

Add the flour and cook over low heat for a few minutes until the flour is cooked but not brown. Remove pan from the heat and add the warm chicken broth, whisking to prevent lumps. Simmer for 5 minutes. Add the blue cheese and stir until smooth. Add the cream and milk and heat to serving temperature. Do not boil, Stir in sherry and pepper just before serving.

This soup is rich, so serve small portions. Sprinkle with chopped chives.

• TIP

If holiday gifts include a wheel of blue cheese, it can be frozen. Cut the wheel into wedges, wrapping each with heavy duty plastic wrap, then overwrap with foil and freeze. It will keep several months and will be perfect in this soup.

• CURRIED PUMPKIN MUSHROOM SOUP

You can throw out any other pumpkin soup recipes you may have clipped out to try. This one is the very best.

My sister tasted it on a visit to Turback's restaurant in Ithaca, N.Y. She wrote "Gourmet" magazine's "You Asked For It" column and asked them to get it for her. The magazine, which tracks down recipes from all over the world, had no trouble getting this one.

When we recreated the soup to precede a wintry wild game dinner both cooks and guests loved it.

The recipe doesn't mention it, but the restaurant serves the soup out of a hollowed pumpkin.

Makes 6 servings

1/2 pound mushrooms, sliced	1 pound can pumpkin puree*
1/2 cup chopped onion	1 tablespoon honey
2 tablespoons unsalted butter	pinch freshly grated nutmeg
2 tablespoons flour	salt and freshly ground black pepper
1 tablespoon curry powder	1 cup whipping cream
3 cups chicken broth	

In a large, heavy saucepan, cook the mushrooms and onion in the butter, stirring over moderate heat, for 3 minutes. The onion should be soft but not brown. Add the flour and curry powder and cook over low heat, stirring constantly, for 5 minutes. Remove pan from the heat, add the stock while whisking. Stir in the pumpkin, honey, nutmeg and salt and pepper to taste. Simmer soup, stirring occasionally for 15 minutes. The recipe can be made ahead to this point.

When ready to serve, heat the soup, and stir in the cream. Heat until the soup is hot, but not boiling.

* Be sure to buy plain pumpkin, not spiced pumpkin pie filling.

5-MINUTE SOUP

While the kettle of soup simmering on the back of the stove has romantic appeal, quick soups are my cup of tea these days.

My sister whips up what she calls 5-minute soup. As she explains, pretty much anything can go in it — leftover meat or chicken, quick-cooking vegetables that are sliced very thin.

The key is that it should resemble a Japanese-style soup, with clear broth and a few vegetables in it. It's a sandwich go-with soup.

Makes 4 servings

2   14½ - ounce cans reduced salt chicken broth
1/2 cup shredded cooked chicken, pork or beef
1/2 cup finely shredded cabbage
1/4 cup thinly sliced, seeded and peeled cucumber
2 green onions, chopped
4 mushrooms, thinly sliced
freshly ground pepper
sesame oil

Bring the broth to a boil in a medium saucepan. Add the remaining ingredients and simmer for 5 minutes. Sprinkle with pepper. Taste and add salt if desired.

Sprinkle a few drops of sesame oil on top of soup before serving.

- *TIP*

Don't overlook the salad bar when picking up ingredients for soup makings. That way you can buy only as much as you need. In an even bigger hurry? Pick up a package of the cabbage and carrot coleslaw makings. One bag's a head start on soup.

• MEXICAN CORN CHOWDER

*Chowders are sustaining soups, meant to fill as well as warm you.
They should be chunky but not artificially thickened as restaurants often do.*

*Corn chowder is one of my favorites, and this is one occasion where the
convenience of canned corn can be put to good use.*

*Made with the kind of staples many people have on hand, it's the perfect
soup to make on a cold and icy weekend when you don't want to leave
the house.*

Makes 6 servings

4 slices bacon, diced	2 1/2 cups milk
2 tablespoons butter	1/2 teaspoon salt
1/2 cup chopped onion	freshly ground black pepper
1/2 teaspoon chili powder	3 canned green chilies
1 12 - ounce can whole	drained, rinsed and diced
kernel corn	2 egg yolks
1 12 - ounce can creamed corn	cheddar cheese

In a small skillet, cook the bacon until crisp; drain on a paper towel. While bacon
cooks, melt the butter in a medium pot and add the onion. Cook over medium heat
until the onion begins to soften. Stir in the chili powder, the corn and 2 cups of the
milk. Add salt and pepper, chilies and bring just to a boil over medium heat.

Blend the egg yolk with remaining 1/2 cup milk and blend in 1/2 cup of the
hot soup.

Remove soup from heat, stir in the egg mixture, return to heat and cook until thick.
Do not let boil.

Serve in soup bowls with a tablespoon grated cheese on top of each. Sprinkle bacon
over soup.

• TIP

Even if salt isn't an issue in your diet, look for canned corn that has 50-percent
reduced salt. It tastes more like corn. In side-by-side tastings, regular canned corn
just tasted like salt.

• *PASTA*

• PASTA PIZZAIOLA

If you're hungering for the taste of pizza but don't want to go out, there's an easy alternative – pasta alla pizzaiola

The Neapolitan sauce, made with tomatoes, olive oil, garlic, onions and seasoned with oregano, has the pizza taste. And you can improvise, adding your favorite pizza ingredients – green peppers or mushrooms.

Makes 4 servings

4 tablespoons olive oil
1 small onion, minced
1 large clove garlic, minced
3 tomatoes, peeled and chopped*
1 teaspoon oregano
salt and freshly ground black pepper

8 ounces rotini or any
   comparable pasta shape
6 ounces grated mozzarella
2 ounces pepperoni, slivered
2 tablespoons freshly grated
Parmesan cheese

In medium-sized pan, saute the onion in the oil until it softens. Add the garlic and stir for 1 minute. Add the chopped tomatoes, oregano, salt to taste and 6-8 grinds of pepper. Cook over medium heat, stirring occasionally, until most of the excess moisture evaporates.

Meanwhile, bring water to a boil in a large pot, add 2 teaspoons salt, and then add the pasta. Cook until it is al dente; just firm to the bite. Drain and return to the pot.

Toss immediately with a little olive oil and mix in the tomato sauce, pepperoni and half the mozzarella cheese.

Pour the mixture into a baking dish and top with remaining cheese. Sprinkle with additional oregano and freshly grated Parmesan cheese and bake in a 400-degree oven for 10 minutes or until bubbling.

*When tomatoes are out of season, use a 14-ounce can of drained Italian plum tomatoes.

• FRESH TOMATO PASTA

Sometimes when I start to cook dinner I remember, vaguely, a recipe I've read, or a restaurant dish I've eaten, or merely a concoction I've heard described.

One I repeatedly read about was pasta with an uncooked sauce of chopped tomatoes, sometimes with basil or bits of cheese. Cold sauce with hot pasta was an intriguing idea.

Now, it has become a summer staple at my house on hot summer nights.

The heat of the pasta just softens the cubes of cheese and the tomatoes retain their wonderful fresh taste. It is not for those who measure the quality of food solely by whether it is piping hot or not.

Makes 2 entree or 4 side- dish servings

4 medium tomatoes
1/4 teaspoon salt
1/4 cup minced onion
12 to 14 leaves fresh basil shredded

1/2 cup soft cheese (such as fontina or brie), cubed
4 tablespoons olive oil
8 ounces pasta

Peel the tomatoes. Cut in half and squeeze out seeds. Dice the tomatoes and place in a small bowl with the salt. Let stand at least half an hour, then drain off excess juice. Mix the tomatoes with the onion, basil, cheese and olive oil.

Bring 2 quarts water to a boil in a large pot; add 2 teaspoons salt. Add the pasta and cook uncovered until done to your liking. Drain the pasta and toss with the sauce.

Serve immediately.

• BAKED TOMATO SAUCE WITH PASTA

The food of Sicily is robust and rustic, and this recipe is a perfect example. It is such an easy-to-make sauce, but a lusty one.

Tomatoes are simply halved – or, if they are large, quartered – and baked with olive oil, garlic, grated cheese and oregano. The soft tomatoes break up as they are tossed with hot pasta. I made some changes in the original recipe reducing the amount of oil, and using Parmesan cheese.

Makes 4 servings

1/2 cup olive oil

1 ¹/₂ pounds fresh
    Roma tomatoes, unpeeled

1/4 cup grated Parmesan cheese

1/4 cup dry bread crumbs

2 cloves garlic, minced

1 teaspoon dried oregano, crumbled

1/4 teaspoon black pepper

1/4 teaspoon salt

1/2 pound penne or similar pasta*

Preheat oven to 400 degrees. Choose a shallow baking dish that will just hold the tomatoes in a single layer. Cover the bottom of a baking dish with the oil. If using Roma tomatoes, cut in half. If using round tomatoes, cut in quarters and flick out the excess seeds. Dip the cut surface of each tomato in the oil, then place in the pan cut side up.

Combine remaining ingredients except pasta and sprinkle over the tomatoes. Bake 40 minutes in middle of the oven. The tomatoes should be very soft.

While tomatoes cook, bring a large pot of salted water to a boil. Cook the pasta al dente and drain. Return to the cooking pot, pour tomatoes and oil over the pasta. Toss and serve with additional grated cheese if desired.

*Penne is a quill shaped pasta. Suitable substitutions include rigatoni and fusilli.

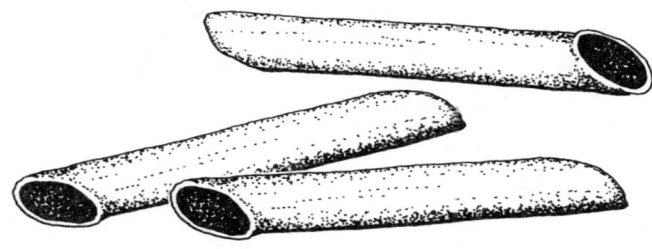

• PASTA WITH ASPARAGUS & HAM

*An old favorite of pasta with fresh asparagus gets a new dimension with the
addition of ham. I particularly like country ham or even proscuitto, which have
more flavor than deli ham. Just be careful with the salt, for ham is salty.*

Makes 2 entree servings

3/4 pound fresh asparagus
8 ounces pasta
4 tablespoons unsalted butter
2 tablespoons minced onion

1/2 cup slivered, cooked country ham
freshly ground black pepper
1/2 cup Parmesan cheese

Trim the asparagus, snapping off woody ends. Cut into 1-inch pieces and drop
into boiling water. Cook uncovered until just tender, drain in a colander and refresh
under cold water. Set aside.

Bring a large pot of water to a boil. Add 2 teaspoons salt and drop in the pasta.
Cook, uncovered, until just tender.

While the pasta cooks, heat 3 tablespoons of the butter in a large skillet. Saute the
onion over medium heat until it is tender; add the ham and asparagus and heat.
Sprinkle in pepper to taste.

Drain the pasta in a colander. Add to the asparagus and ham with the remaining
tablespoon of butter. Toss with cheese just before serving.

• PASTA WITH BUTTER-WINE SAUCE

John Rossi not only makes pasta distributed across the country in his name, he's an inventive cook as well. In his butter days, he used to give out this recipe. He still should, for it is a lovely pasta dish that's wonderfully quick to fix. And while we all eat butter with restraint these days, there are places for it. This is one.

Because the ingredients are so few, it's important to choose top quality: unsalted butter, a good white wine, Parmigiano Reggiano cheese and fresh herbs from the garden. Try parsley or chives or basil. I liked Rossi's angel hair pasta with this sauce, which is redolent of wine.

Start the sauce when you put the pasta water on to boil. If you use Rossi pasta, which cooks quickly, the whole dish will be done in less than 10 minutes.

Makes 4 to 6 first course or side-dish servings

1 stick unsalted butter	12 ounces pasta
1 tablespoon olive oil	1/2 cup grated Parmesan cheese
1/2 medium onion, minced	1/4 cup minced fresh herbs
1 cup dry white wine	

Put a large pot of salted water on to boil.

In a large skillet, melt the butter with the oil. Add the minced onion and cook over medium heat until the onion softens but does not brown.

Add the wine and cook for 2 to 3 minutes.

Cook the pasta according to package directions. When just done, drain in a colander and add immediately to the skillet. Toss the pasta with the butter-wine sauce to coat thoroughly. Add half the cheese and herbs and toss again.

Serve with remaining cheese sprinkled on top.

• BUTTERFLIES & BEANS

I don't know if it was the picture or the name that caught my eye when I first spotted this recipe for butterflies and beans.

The "butterflies" are pasta bow-ties, which also look a little like butterflies. The picture promised a colorful dish of pasta with green beans and a sauce made with plenty of green herbs and spinach.

The recipe lived up to its picture promise.

Makes 4 servings

3/4 pound green beans,
   cut into 1/2-inch pieces
1/2 cup fresh basil leaves
1/2 cup fresh parsley leaves
1 clove garlic,
   coarsely chopped
1 tablespoon chopped
   fresh chives

1/8 teaspoon crushed
   dried rosemary
1/3 cup grated Parmesan cheese
3 tablespoons olive oil
2 tablespoons chicken stock
2 fresh spinach leaves
3/4 pound pasta butterflies
   (or bow ties), cooked

Steam beans until tender.

In a food processor or blender, combine basil, parsley, garlic, chives, rosemary and cheese. Process until chopped. Add oil, stock and spinach and process until smooth.

In a warm serving bowl, combine beans and cooked pasta. Add sauce and toss gently. Serve immediately.

• RIGATONI WITH ROASTED RED PEPPERS

Pasta is here to stay, a staple in our diets. No one can have too many pasta recipes.

This favorite of mine relies on roasted red peppers, which can be very expensive out of season. That's why I urge people to put up their own in August.

Makes 6 appetizer servings

4 roasted red bell peppers	1/2 teaspoon salt
1/2 cup olive oil	1/4 teaspoon ground black pepper
2 tablespoons tiny black olives	12 ounces rigatoni
1 garlic clove, bruised	1/4 cup toasted pine nuts
1/2 teaspoon oregano	large shavings Parmesan cheese*

Cut the peppers into strips. Combine with the oil, olives, garlic, oregano, salt and pepper. Cover and marinate at room temperature 1 to 2 hours, or refrigerate overnight.

Cook the pasta in a large pot of boiling, salted water until firm to the bite, about 12 minutes. Remove garlic from the peppers; toss the peppers with the pasta. Arrange on warmed individual plates, sprinkle with the pine nuts and Parmesan cheese.

* Use a cheese plane to get the large shavings.

• SPAGHETTINI CASINO

Spaghettini "casino" with clams and bacon is a cross between spaghetti with white clam sauce and clams casino. It is a quick supper – the sauce can be made while the pasta cooks.

Most of the inland world will have to use canned clams for this recipe. Please buy the best. Reese brand or 3-Diamond brand chopped clams taste like clams packed in clam juice, unlike some other brands that are packed in a yellow liquid. If you can only buy the cheaper variety, don't use the juice.

Makes 2 servings

2 to 4 slices bacon	1/2 pound spaghettini
1 dozen clams (or 1 cup, shucked)*	2 large pats butter
2 tablespoons olive oil	2 tablespoons fresh parsley,
1 large clove garlic, minced	minced
Red pepper flakes	

Put about 4 quarts salted water on to boil. Cut bacon slices in half and fry very slowly until just crisp; drain on paper towels and reserve.

If using freshly shucked clams, chop coarsely and save the juices. Heat the olive oil in a small, heavy skillet and saute the garlic a few minutes on low heat. Add pepper flakes (a few shakes from the spice bottle) and turn off heat.

Cook the spaghettini al dente, drain, add butter and place in hot bowls. Keep warm in a low oven. Turn the heat back on under the skillet and toss in the clams and the parsley and a little of the juice. Stir around until the clams are just heated through and barely cooked, about 1 minute.

Divide the clams between the waiting bowls of pasta and crumble the reserved bacon over the top of each serving.

*You'll need two cans for 1 cup clams.

• HIGHLAND PASTA

My guests asked what the first course was and I only told them pasta with smoked salmon. They detected a mystery ingredient but couldn't identify the source of the flavor.

It was scotch, and even though none of these friends are scotch drinkers, they loved the taste that becomes elusive in this sauce.

Don't turn up your nose at the notion of scotch in the pasta. In the late '80s the trendy pasta dish had vodka in the sauce. And think of all the dishes flamed with brandy and even gin. You won't taste the scotch, just the smoky taste that some say comes from Scotland's peat.

Because of the cream, this dish is indulgently rich and best served as an appetizer rather than a main course.

Makes 4 appetizer servings

8 ounces pasta shells or wheels	1/3 cup scotch
2 green onions, finely chopped	2 tablespoons lemon juice
2 tablespoons butter	freshly ground black pepper
4 ounces smoked salmon, diced	2 tablespoons mixture of chopped
1 cup whipping cream	fresh chives and parsley

Put the pasta on to cook in boiling salted water 8 or 9 minutes. At the same time, saute the green onions in the butter until soft but not brown. Add the salmon; saute for 2 minutes, stirring. Add the cream, scotch and lemon juice and simmer for 4 or 5 minutes to thicken the sauce. Grind pepper over drained pasta. Sprinkle with half the herbs and toss with sauce. Arrange pasta on individual plates and sprinkle with remaining herbs.

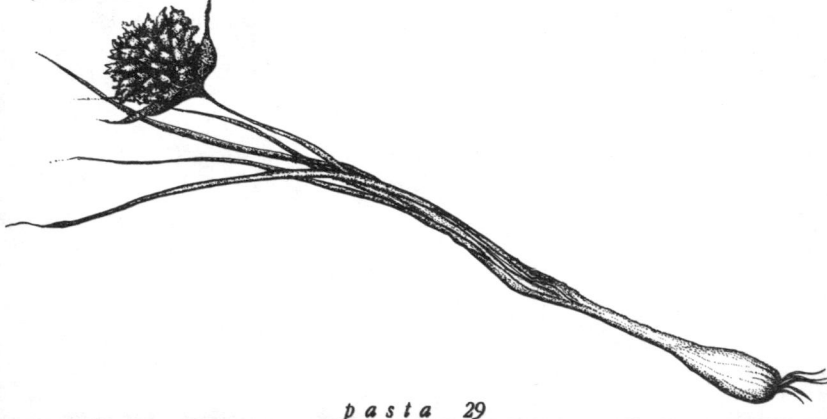

• MADAME'S NOODLES

Times – and eating habits – change but memories stand still. And my memory of Madame's noodles is vivid. Call her recipe a testimonial to the way we once cooked and occasionally still do.

The recipe, from the 1980 edition of "It's Simple", came from French cooking teacher Madame Liane Kuony. We toiled in the classes and never got around to making this dish, which she fixed for us once, but later she passed on the recipe.

It is a wonderful, rich side dish, but it must be finished at the last minute and served while steaming hot – like most pasta and cheese dishes, the noodles will begin to stick together if they cool.

Makes 6 servings

1 cup light (coffee) cream heated	4 quarts water
1 ½ sticks butter, softened	1 generous cup grated Swiss cheese
12-ounce package noodles	1 large clove garlic, minced
4 heaping teaspoons salt	1/2 cup fresh parsley, minced

Put the butter and hot cream in a large mixing bowl and set it over a pasta pot containing steaming water until butter melts. Cook the noodles in salted water just until done (bite through one to test). Drain the noodles, and quickly add them to the bowl with the cream and butter. Toss until the noodles are creamy.

Add the cheese, garlic and parsley and toss until the cheese melts and strings. Serve immediately.

• *JAPANESE NOODLE SALAD*

This noodle salad is excellent for summer. It can be ready in 10 or 15 minutes if you buy cooked chicken at the supermarket deli. The recipe is loosely adapted from a Japanese somen salad; A traditional version also would include strips of cooked eggs.

Makes 2 servings

2 servings fresh, pre-cooked yaki-soba noodles
1 teaspoon sesame oil
1/2 small head romaine
sesame seed dressing (recipe follows)
4 green onions, finely chopped
2 cooked chicken breasts, skinned and shredded
2 tablespoons fresh cilantro

Put noodles in a colander. Pour a teakettle full of boiling water over the noodles, tossing with a fork to separate noodles. Rinse the noodles with cool water, drain and toss with sesame oil.

Slice lettuce, crosswise, into thin shreds. Combine half the dressing with the noodles and onions.

On two plates, make a bed of the lettuce. Arrange the noodles on the lettuce and top with the chicken. Drizzle remaining dressing over and sprinkle with cilantro.

• *SESAME SEED DRESSING*

2 tablespoons sesame seed, toasted
2 tablespoons sugar
1 teaspoon salt
3 tablespoons rice vinegar

2 tablespoons soy sauce
1/4 teaspoon freshly grated
    ginger root
1/4 cup vegetable oil

Combine all ingredients in a small covered jar and shake well.

• *POULTRY*

• BUTTERMILK FRIED CHICKEN BREASTS

Pan frying chicken; standing at the skillet and turning the chicken to achieve a proper brown hue, is time consuming.

But adaptations can be made. Using boneless chicken breasts cuts the cooking time to 8 to 10 minutes. And in this variation, a buttermilk marinade produces chicken that is very moist and tender – if you don't overcook it.

Be sure to use Louisiana hot sauce, sold under various labels, which is milder than Tabasco. While the amount seems generous, the hot sauce makes the chicken flavorful, not overly spicy.

Makes 4 servings

4 large, boneless, skinless chicken breast halves
2 cups buttermilk
1/2 cup Louisiana hot sauce
2 teaspoons salt
1 cup flour
freshly ground black pepper
1 tablespoon each vegetable oil and butter

Flatten the breasts slightly with a meat mallet. Put the chicken, buttermilk, hot sauce and 1 teaspoon of the salt in a plastic bag and marinate at room temperature for 1 hour.

Combine the flour and the remaining 1 teaspoon salt and 8 to 10 grinds of pepper.

Just before cooking, heat the butter and oil in a large skillet. Remove the chicken from the marinade, pat dry with paper towels and roll in the flour, shaking off excess. Cook the chicken 8 to 10 minutes over medium high heat until brown on both sides and cooked through to a temperature of 165 degrees.

• TIP

For later convenience, add 4 more breasts to the marinade, seal the bag and freeze. When thawed, the chicken is ready to cook.

• LEMON ROAST CHICKEN

The most popular recipe I ever printed may be this one for lemon roast chicken, which was included in the 1980 edition of "It's Simple".

It's a recipe from Marcella Hazan, whose cooking schools in Italy and New York educated thousands of American cooks to authentic Italian home cooking.

The first recipe of hers that I sampled is this roast chicken with lemon. It turned out to be unbelievably simple and delicious.

Makes 4 servings

1 chicken, about 2 ½ to 3 pounds
salt and pepper
2 whole lemons

Wash the chicken, drain and dry it with paper towels. Remove any loose fat. Sprinkle with salt and pepper, inside and out, rubbing it in.

Wash and dry the lemons and soften by rolling them on the counter. Poke each lemon at least 20 times with a skewer, ice pick or toothpick. Put the lemons inside the chicken, close the opening with toothpicks or skewers and loosely tie the legs together.

Put in a roasting pan, breast down and put in the upper third of an oven preheated to 350 degrees. Do not add any fat.

After 15 minutes, turn chicken breast up and roast another 20 to 25 minutes. Turn the heat to 400 degrees and cook chicken an additional 20 minutes. (If using a larger bird, you may want to roast the bird an additional 5 minutes or so-cut into the thigh at the joint and make sure the juices run clear yellow.)

Serve the chicken with all the lemony juices in the roasting pan. They make a delicious sauce.

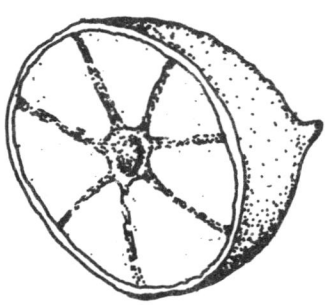

• SAUTEED CHICKEN WITH SPAGHETTI

Most kitchen gadgets end up at the back of the drawer, but a few are essential to making life easier on the cook.

One is a rotary grater that makes quick work of grating cheese and nuts. The other is a zester for which there is no substitute.

Lemon zest is the central flavoring in this recipe I adapted from a dish at Joyce Goldstein's Square One restaurant in San Francisco. She uses fresh tuna but I use chicken, which is cheaper.

Makes 2 servings

1 large onion, peeled and halved
4 tablespoons olive oil
1/2 small dried red chili
2 tablespoons lemon zest
1 tablespoon lemon juice
4 teaspoons minced garlic

2 teaspoons capers, chopped
salt and freshly ground pepper
2 boneless, skinless chicken
  breast halves
8 ounces spaghetti, cooked
2 tablespoons minced parsley

Put onions cut side down and sliver vertically. In a medium saucepan, heat 3 tablespoons of the oil over medium heat. Add chili and onion and cook until tender but not soft. Stir in the lemon zest and juice, garlic and capers and season with salt and pepper to taste.

Heat remaining oil in a skillet over medium-high heat. Sprinkle chicken with salt and pepper and cook, turning once, until brown and cooked through, 8 to 10 minutes depending on the thickness of the breast.

Toss the sauce with the cooked spaghetti. Slice the chicken on the diagonal and serve on top of the spaghetti. Sprinkle with parsley.

• BAKED CHICKEN WITH WHITE WINE & ROSEMARY

Rosemary is one of the pungent herbs that people are passionate about. My father, who didn't like it, referred to it as Mary Jane and I never got around to telling him what THAT meant.

I prefer to use fresh rosemary, because the needles are soft. While flavor of dried rosemary is good, it never seems to soften, no matter how long it has cooked. If you must use dried, use half the amount.

This simple recipe provides a good introduction to rosemary. The amounts can be increased easily to serve more people. Don't discard the pan juices. Spoon a little over each serving.

Makes 4 servings

four pieces chicken*	1/4 cup soy sauce
1/2 cup white wine	1 teaspoon fresh rosemary leaves, snipped

Put the chicken in a shallow baking dish just large enough to accommodate the chicken. Mix the wine and soy sauce and pour over the chicken. Sprinkle the rosemary leaves over.

Bake uncovered at 350 degrees for 50 minutes, basting with the liquid every 15 minutes. Put a few sprigs of rosemary around the platter before serving.

*Use either legs, including both drumsticks and thighs, or breasts, on the bone. Breast meat will cook in less time. Size varies dramatically; small ones will cook in as little as 25 minutes. Figure on 35 to 40 minutes for very large ones. If you have an instant-read thermometer, remove from oven when white meat is cooked to 160 to 165 degrees, dark meat to 170 to 175. The temperature will continue to rise.

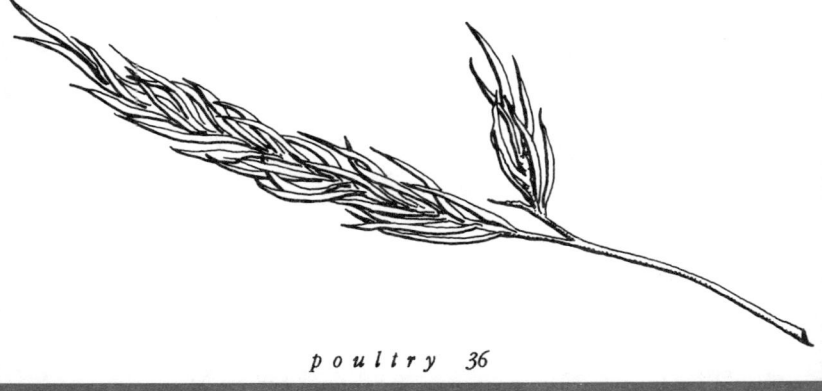

• *CHICKEN WITH SHIITAKE MUSHROOMS*

Time was when mushrooms in a recipe referred to plain button mushrooms. But these days supermarkets offer a range of mushrooms from delicate, long-stemmed enoki to the flavorful shiitake mushrooms.

When chefs use them, they often list them on the menu as wild mushrooms, but actually they're farm-raised

Makes 4 servings

1/4 pound shiitake mushrooms
1 pound chicken breasts, boned
   and skinned
1 clove garlic, halved
3 tablespoons flour

1/4 cup butter
1/2 teaspoon salt
freshly ground black pepper
1/3 cup dry white wine
1/2 cup cream

Remove tough stems from mushrooms. Wipe caps clean with a dampened paper towel and cut into 1/4-inch strips. Set aside.

Flatten chicken breasts with a mallet and rub with cut side of garlic. Cut into 1/2-inch strips. Sprinkle the chicken strips with flour and toss in a colander to remove excess flour.

Heat butter in a large skillet. Add chicken and saute over medium high heat to brown lightly. Stir to separate strips. Add the mushrooms strips, salt and pepper and mix well. Add the wine, cover and cook 8 to 10 minutes. Add cream and raise the heat to reduce and thicken sauce. Sprinkle with parsley and serve with pasta.

• CHICKEN IN MANY MUSTARDS

Chicken is every cook's answer to the quick fix. Marinades, started ahead, add flavor and do their work while we work or play.

On weekdays, starting a fire in the grill may seem like too much trouble, but the marinated chicken is ready to cook and you can concentrate on other parts of the meal while the flames die down to a proper bed of coals. Chicken breasts on the bone take 25 to 30 minutes to cook. To cut time even further, use boned, skinless breasts and cook on an open grill, only 5-6 minutes per side.

Makes 4 servings

1/4 cup Dijon mustard	1/2 cup apple juice
1/4 cup whole seed mustard	juice of 1/2 lemon
1/4 cup hot mustard	1 whole shallot or onion, sliced
1/4 cup white vinegar	freshly ground black pepper
1/4 cup olive oil	4 chicken breast halves, on the bone

Combine all ingredients, except chicken, in a large bowl and whisk to emulsify. Put chicken in marinade and mix well with hands to thoroughly coat pieces. Marinate at room temperature for 2 hours (or in the refrigerator for up to 48 hours).

Lay a charcoal fire and when the coals are ready, place chicken on the grill, skin- side down. Cover and cook for 15 minutes; turn and cook another 10 to15 minutes.

• SOUTHWEST CHILI CHICKEN

What the weekday cook really needs to do is plan ahead, though that's difficult for those of us who like to take life one day at a time.

This chicken gets the benefit of a marinade whipped up in the morning — or the night before. The chicken tastes best on the grill but it can be baked or broiled. If you like spicy food, add hot sauce to the marinade.

As an alternative, remove the skin and top with a little smoked cheese for the last 5 minutes.

Makes 4 servings

4 large chicken breasts,
  about 2 ½ pounds
1/4 cup lime juice
2 teaspoons chili powder
1 teaspoon salt
1 clove garlic, minced

1/4 teaspoon pepper
1/4 cup olive oil
1/3 cup minced fresh cilantro
  or parsley

Rinse the chicken and remove any excess fat. Leave the skin on while cooking.

Blend the lime juice, chili powder, salt, garlic and pepper in a mini food processor. Add the oil and blend thoroughly

Place the chicken in a single layer in a baking dish and pour the marinade over, turning to coat both sides. Cover and refrigerate 8 to 24 hours.

If you choose, grill the chicken breasts over medium hot coals, turning several times, for about 25 minutes, until cooked through and no pink remains at the bone.

The easier approach is to bake the drained chicken, uncovered at 400 degrees for 30 to 40 minutes, depending on the size of the breasts.

Sprinkle with cilantro or parsley before serving.

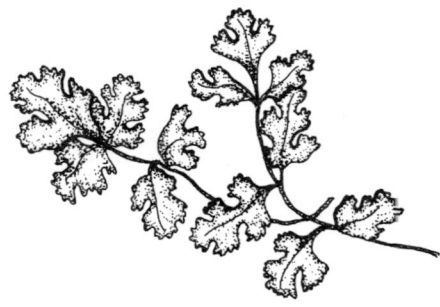

• MEXICAN GRILLED CHICKEN

Hot weather and hot food go together. You doubt it? Why else would countries such as Mexico and Thailand have wedded their cuisines to the chili pepper?

Our experience with those spicy cuisines has been limited, of necessity, by the unavailability of the array of peppers. But these days there are more than jalapeno peppers at the produce counter.

Fresh chilies are essential for the salsa served with this recipe. The chicken itself is not highly seasoned.

Makes 4 servings

1 cup white vinegar
1/2 cup water
2 small cloves garlic,
    crushed and chopped
2 $1/_2$ teaspoons salt
1 $1/_2$ teaspoons mild chili powder

1/2 teaspoon toasted oregano*
1/2 teaspoon black pepper
1 bay leaf
1 5-pound chicken, cut into
    quarters, washed and dried
Salsa Pico de Gallo (see index)

Combine all the ingredients for the marinade and pour over chicken; cover and marinate in the refrigerator for 3 hours, turning once.

Bring to room temperature; remove from marinade and grill over hot coals, turning for 35 to 40 minutes. Cook dark meat another 5 minutes. Serve with Salsa Pico de Gallo and warm tortillas.

* Toast spices in a dry skillet until aromatic, about one minute.

• TURKEY HASH

As sure as Thanksgiving comes every year, there are leftovers. Maybe some pie, probably some cranberry sauce and mashed potatoes that can be recycled as a kind of potato pancake or into fluffy rolls. And, most certainly, turkey. I relish the cold meat for sandwiches and the carcass for soup. When I can, I save enough meat for turkey hash, which is every bit as good as turkey the first time around.

Makes 4 servings

3 tablespoons butter
1 small onion, minced (about 1/2 cup)
1 green pepper, diced
3 to 4 cups turkey, cubed

1/3 cup slivered almonds
1/2 cup cream
salt and pepper

Melt the butter in a 9-inch skillet. Add the onion and green pepper and saute over medium heat until the vegetables soften slightly.

Add the turkey and almonds; stir and saute, allowing the turkey to brown a bit. Pour the cream over the turkey and cook until the cream is absorbed. Season with salt and pepper to taste.

Serve with a simple green salad for a light supper.

NOTE: Instead of incorporating the nuts in the turkey mixture, you can also brown the almonds in a tablespoon of butter and sprinkle them over the turkey hash before serving.

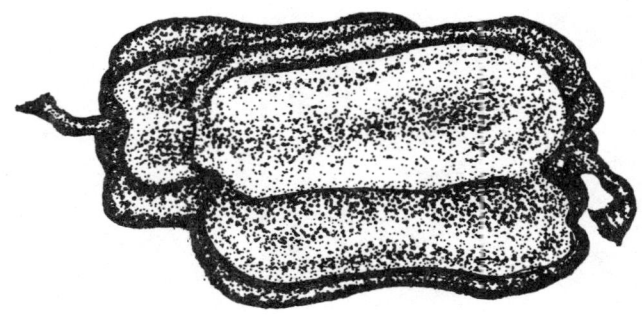

• SMOKED TURKEY

As interest in turkey continues to grow, we've gotten beyond eating the bird just at Thanksgiving and Christmas. Other times of the year, when it's not so cold outside, turkey is excellent on the grill.

Cooking a turkey breast in a covered grill is a minimum-fuss way to entertain. No basting is required. All you have to do is check occasionally to see that the fire is properly stoked. You'll end up with a golden brown, moist and slightly smoky bird. It's best when allowed to cool a bit.

Makes 10 to 12 servings

2 handfuls wood chips*
1 whole turkey breast, 6 to 8 pounds, on the bone
salt

Soak the chips in water for at least 20 minutes. With the vents open on the grill, build a fire for the indirect method of cooking. That means to arrange the hot coals around a drip pan about the size of the turkey. When the coals are covered with a gray ash, add the chips, well drained, to the charcoal. Sprinkle turkey with salt and place on the grill, bone side down, above the drip pan. Put the cover on the grill and cook the turkey 11 to 13 minutes per pound (more time may be required on a damp or windy day). Replenish coals as needed, adding briquets around the sides.

It's best to check the turkey with a meat thermometer. The National Turkey Federation recommends removing the turkey when the temperature is 165 degrees. (The temperature will rise to 170 as a result of residual heat.) Many professional cooks would suggest removing it from the grill at 160 degrees.

*Try apple wood chips or hickory.

• CURRIED TURKEY TENDERLOINS

Recipes are sometimes developed by the seat of my pants. This one evolved from a salmon recipe I was working on.

This recipe is very quick to prepare. It's hot with curry and sweet from the orange juice and red bell peppers. Serve it with fresh basil or cilantro, if you like.

Makes 2 to 3 servings

1 pound turkey tenderloins
2 tablespoons curry powder
2 teaspoons ground cumin
1/2 teaspoon salt
1/2 teaspoon ground pepper

peanut or vegetable oil
1 clove garlic, sliced in half
1 red bell pepper, cored and chopped
1 orange, juiced
1/4 cup slivered fresh basil

Cut the tenderloin on the diagonal into slices 1/2-inch thick. Flatten slightly with a meat mallet.

Combine the curry, cumin, salt and pepper. Roll the turkey in the seasoning mix.

Spray oil – or heat 1 tablespoon oil – in a large skillet. Add garlic and heat over a medium flame, just until the garlic is light brown. Discard garlic and add seasoned turkey slices. Cook 4 minutes and turn. Add the diced pepper and cook another 4 minutes.

Add the orange juice and boil for a minute or two until it forms a thick glaze. Stir in basil. Serve immediately, with a spoonful of the sauce.

• *MEATS*

• ROAST PORK TENDERLOIN

Pork tenderloin is my preferred cut of the pig. It's more expensive, but it's tender, boneless and lean.

Since I began writing "It's Simple", advice on cooking pork has changed. USDA guidelines used to say to cook pork to 180 degrees, which was lowered to 170 degrees and, more recently, 160 degrees. The meat will be slightly pink. The change is necessary to keep the meat moist because so much fat has been bred out of the pig.

The National Pork Producers Council, which is actively promoting the change, also suggests cooking this cut at a high temperature. Here's my favorite recipe, revised.

Makes 2 to 3 servings

1 pork tenderloin, about 3/4 pound*	1 teaspoon minced fresh rosemary
1/2 teaspoon coarse salt	1 teaspoon olive oil
1 small clove garlic	freshly ground black pepper

Preheat the oven to 450 degrees. Fold the slender tip of the meat under so it will cook evenly. Tie or skewer the tip in place. Place on a foil-lined broiling pan.

Mash the garlic and salt together in a mortar and pestle until it forms a paste. Blend in the rosemary and oil.

Rub the paste into the meat and sprinkle with freshly ground pepper. Roast for 20 minutes. Remove from the oven at 155 degrees. If necessary, return meat to the oven for another 5 minutes.

Let it stand, lightly covered with foil, for 10 minutes. The internal temperature will rise to 160 degrees. Slice and serve with any pan juices.

*The vacuum-packed tenderloins often come two to a package; fix both and save one to slice and eat cold.

• TIP

To be sure of meat temperatures, buy an instant-read meat thermometer, which sell as low as $10. The internal temperature of the meat registers in seconds, eliminating guesswork.

• SPANISH PORK LOIN

One of my favorite Spanish recipes is this incredibly easy seasoned pork loin.

The pork is slathered with a mixture of paprika, garlic and herbs and left to marinate for several days.

This is a wonderful piece of meat to have on hand, and it can be kept refrigerated for several days. If you don't use it all at one time, the pork is a flavorful substitute for bacon in a BLT.

Makes 4 to 6 servings

1 tablespoon paprika	1 teaspoon coarse salt
2 cloves garlic, crushed	1 bay leaf, broken
3 tablespoons olive oil	1 $\frac{1}{2}$ pounds boneless pork loin
1/4 teaspoon dried thyme	oil for frying

In a small bowl mix paprika, garlic, oil, thyme and salt to a paste. Spread the mixture on the pork and rub it in, coating all sides. Place in a glass dish with the bay leaf, cover well and refrigerate at least overnight. The meat will be more flavorful after several days.

To serve, slice the meat into quarter-inch slices. Heat a little oil in a skillet and saute the slices, about 2 minutes on each side. Remove the meat and deglaze the pan with 2 to 3 tablespoons white wine or chicken broth or water. Stir up all the pan juices and pour a little sauce over the meat.

If making sandwiches, skip the last step.

• GINGER PORK

One of the best pork dishes I've ever fixed is this ginger pork. The meat is exquisitely tender and the flavor simply lovely.

The dish is so simple, it qualifies for entry into my collection of 15-minute meals. While the dish is Japanese in style, it relies on ingredients available at the supermarket. The key is the seemingly extravagant amount of ginger. It's important that the ginger is grated, not minced.

Makes 4 servings

1 ½ pounds pork tenderloin
3 tablespoons sake*
5 tablespoons light soy sauce

1 (4-inch) section fresh ginger root
2 tablespoons vegetable oil
flour

Cut the tenderloin, on the diagonal, into slices 1/4-inch thick. You should have 20 to 24 slices. Combine sake or vermouth and soy sauce. Grate the ginger; there should be about 3-4 tablespoons pulp and juice. Add to the sake and combine with the pork and let marinate 5 to 6 minutes.

Heat the oil in the skillet. While the oil heats, pat meat dry with paper towels and dust the meat lightly with flour, shaking off any excess. Saute the meat, in batches, over medium-high heat until both sides are golden. Do not overcook. Keep the first batch warm on a serving plate while you cook the remaining pork.

*In a pinch, use dry sherry or vermouth.

• TIP

Metal ginger graters, designed just for this purpose, are available in Japanese food stores.

• GRILLED PORK CHOPS

Forget about barbecued pork chops. The best I've ever had were un-touched by traditional barbecue sauce.

The treat, served by the Ohio Pork Producers council to food editors at a picnic at Michael Farms near Urbana was simplicity itself: very thick pork chops, cut 1 ¹/₄-inch thick, grilled slowly and basted with a tart mixture of vinegar, Worcestershire sauce, oil and salt. It's a variation of what is called mop sauce in some parts of the country. It's used while the meat cooks, unlike tomato-based sauces, which should be applied only at the end of the cooking time.

Mix up a six-cup batch of the basting liquid and keep it on hand for bar-becues. The best way to apply it to the chops is with a spray bottle. Remem-ber, it's important to use thick chops and to cook them slowly. Ask the butcher to cut them for you. Figure on one hefty chop per person.

Makes 4 servings

2 cups cider vinegar	2 tablespoons Worcestershire sauce
2 cups vegetable oil	2 tablespoons salt
2 cups water	4 center-cut pork chops, 1¹/₄ inches thick

Blend the vinegar, oil, water, Worcestershire and salt. This will make six cups. Put a cup or so in a plastic spray bottle. Have a charcoal fire or gas grill ready. Cook the chops over medium, not hot, coals, turning frequently and spraying with the mop sauce for about 35 to 40 minutes. Reserve any remaining sauce for another cookout.

• SAUSAGE & APPLES

Fall is Ohio's brief season of glory. The leaves turn, the sky is brilliant blue, and farm markets set out their colorful crops of squash and pumpkins and apples.

Crisp nights whet appetites for substantial fare such as this dinner of sausage and apples.

This is a flexible recipe, easily adapted for additional people. Figure on two 4-inch chunks of sausage for people with hearty appetites, and generally put in one apple per person.

It's important to use crisp, tart, cooking apples, not mushy, tasteless Red Delicious. Go to a farm market where the selection is wider than what local supermarkets offer.

Makes 4 servings

4 large, tart, cooking apples	3/4 cup dry white wine
4 teaspoons unsalted butter	2 ounces brandy (optional)
1 $\frac{1}{2}$ pounds smoked sausage, cut in eight chunks	

Peel and core the apples. Slice in 1/2-inch thick slices. Melt the butter in a large, heavy skillet over medium heat. Add the apples and sausage chunks to the pan. Cook, stirring apples occasionally and turning sausage, for 12 to 15 minutes. The apples should brown lightly and become soft, but not mushy.

Remove the sausage and apples to a serving dish. Add wine and optional brandy to the skillet. Raise heat, and stir the boiling liquid to dissolve the good pan juices. When the liquid is reduced by half, pour over the apples.

Serve with plain boiled or steamed potatoes. Or, for a more substantial meal, with sauerkraut and mashed potatoes.

• *POTATOES, PEPPERS & SAUSAGE*

One of the easiest one-dish suppers I know is this robustly flavored mixture of potatoes, peppers, onion and sausage. It's easy to fix after work and before whatever is scheduled that evening and will feed a family of four nicely. It can easily be cut in half to serve two.

If you use thin-skinned new potatoes, don't peel them. That helps cut down on time spent in the kitchen.

Makes 4 servings

1 pound sausage*	1 large onion
1 ¹/₂ pounds green peppers	1/4 cup good olive oil
1 pound new potatoes	salt and freshly ground black pepper

Preheat oven to 425 degrees. Prick sausages and blanch in simmering water briefly to remove excess fat. Trim peppers, removing seeds and cut into rough, 1-inch sections. Wash potatoes and cut into 1-inch cubes. Cut onion into similar-sized cubes.

Pile vegetables into a shallow casserole. Drizzle oil over and mix to coat the vegetables. Sprinkle with salt and pepper and top with sausages.

Bake for 30 minutes, stirring several times until potatoes are tender.

* Mettwurst, Polish or Italian sausage is suitable. If desired, cut into sections before adding to potatoes.

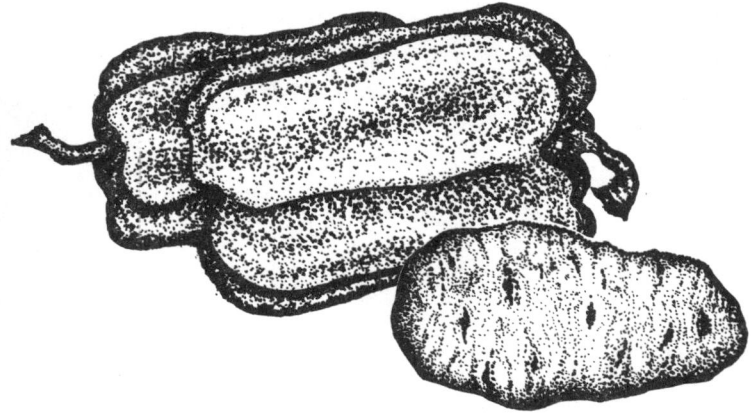

• GREEK-STYLE STEAK

I know you say you don't like anchovies. But what you don't know is that chefs often slip them into their creations unannounced.

Mashed down until they're invisible in a sauce, the anchovies add body and flavor that no one will identify.

Quality of anchovies varies, and the more expensive ones packed in glass are indeed better. If you settle for the tinned variety, soak them in milk for a half hour to reduce the fishiness.

Try them in this steak marinade, which can be started in the morning or the night before.

Makes 2 servings

2 tablespoons olive oil
1 tablespoon slivered garlic
3 anchovies, chopped

1/2 tablespoon fresh rosemary, snipped
1/2 cup red wine
2 sirloin tip steaks, 3/4-inch thick*

In a small skillet, heat the oil and garlic over a medium flame. When the garlic begins to sizzle, add the anchovies and stir, mashing the anchovies into the sauce. Cook just until the garlic is golden, not brown or it will become bitter. Add the rosemary and remove from the heat. Add the wine and let the mixture cool. Pour over the steaks and let marinate for 8 hours but no more than 24.

Grill or pan-fry the steaks for a total of 5 to 6 minutes for medium rare.

*This marinade also works well with flank steak. Marinate for 24 hours.

• *TIP*

Look for packages of fresh rosemary in supermarket produce sections. Potted rosemary plants do well in the house over winter providing an ample and inexpensive supply.

• ROAST BEEF WITH
PASTA & ONION SAUCE

Sunday afternoons are the perfect time to tuck a roast in the oven. This aromatic roast cooks slowly on top of lots of onions. Combining the soft onions and the meat juices produces an instant sauce for a side of spaghetti.

Makes 4 to 6 servings

2 -pound rump roast
salt and freshly ground
   black pepper
1 tablespoon olive oil
2 pounds onions, peeled and
   sliced 1/2-inch thick

8 cloves garlic, peeled
10 ounces spaghetti
3/4 cup grated Parmesan cheese
1/4 cup minced fresh
   chives or parsley

Preheat oven to 250 degrees.

Season the meat with salt and pepper. Drizzle oil over bottom of a cast iron or enameled Dutch oven. Place the onion slices in bottom of the pan and sprinkle with salt and pepper. Add garlic cloves and top with the meat, fat side up.

Cover, making sure pot is well sealed. Cook in the oven for 5 hours, turning the meat once or twice. Remove the pan from the oven and place meat on a serving plate. You can serve the roast as is, surrounded by the onions.

For a pasta side dish, first put the meat and half the onions on a serving platter, cover with foil and place in the turned-off oven to keep warm.

Put the remaining onions in a food processor with the meat juices and chop coarsely. Do not puree.

Cook the spaghetti according to package directions. Drain and toss with the onion sauce and stir over low heat for 1 minute. Sprinkle generously with pepper, the cheese and fresh herbs.

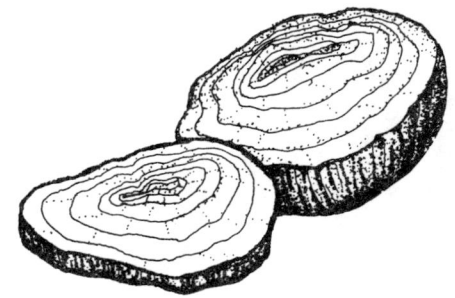

• FLANK STEAK DIJON

One of the most attractive cuts of beef, from a health-conscious point of view, is lean, virtually fat-free flank steak.

It is not a cut of meat for those who like their meat cooked well done because, without any fat, the flank steak gets tough if cooked more than medium rare.

But that means it cooks quickly, in about 8 to 12 minutes on a hot grill. Advance preparation, in the form of a marinade, is essential. This one adds a healthy dose of coarse-grained mustard to a basic vinegar-and-oil marinade. It's a great combination for those who like mustard with beef.

Makes 4 to 6 servings

1/4 cup coarse-grind
 Dijon mustard
2 tablespoons vinegar
2 tablespoons olive oil
1 clove garlic, crushed
 in a garlic press

2 teaspoons minced
 fresh parsley
3/4 teaspoon pepper
1 flank steak, 1 ½ pounds
salt

Combine the mustard and vinegar and whisk in the oil. Add the garlic, parsley and pepper and mix.

Spread the mixture over both sides of the flank steak and marinate, in the refrigerator, for at least 6 hours.

Grill the steak over hot coals. The timing depends on the thickness of the steak, but begin with 5 minutes on one side and 3 to 4 minutes on the other. Do not cook beyond medium rare.

Slice on the diagonal and sprinkle with coarse salt before serving.

• OUR BEST HAMBURGER

When food consultant Howard Solganik and I set out to make the best hamburger we could, we tried all kinds of beef and experimented with seasonings.

The best hamburger was made with ground chuck. We seasoned it with a little minced onion and garlic, but not so much that it overwhelmed the taste of the beef. We added a few dashes of Tabasco.

And, borrowing from an old James Beard recipe for hamburgers, we added a bit of cream. The cholesterol and fat watchers will faint, but it makes a wonderful hamburger. The cream adds moisture and distributes the flavor components throughout each patty.

We made thick, but not enormous patties; about three to a pound and about 3/4-inch thick. We cooked them over a hardwood charcoal fire. We served it on a toasted, chewy, onion roll. And we added a touch of home-made salsa. Maybe by skipping the mayo and cheese, we made up for that added cream. Here's our recipe:

Makes 3 to 4 patties

1 pound choice ground chuck
1 clove garlic, minced
   (about 1/2 teaspoon)
1/2 small onion, minced
   (about 2 tablespoons)

1 tablespoon cream
2 dashes Tabasco
1/2 teaspoon salt
   freshly ground black pepper

Combine all ingredients and mix very gently. With minimal handling, shape the beef into 3 or 4 patties. Grill over medium-hot coals, turning once, for a total of 9 to 10 minutes for a burger that's still pink inside. Cooking time varies depending on distance from the coals, temperature of the coals, and the temperature and thickness of the meat.

Serve on a toasted bun with homemade salsa.

- *NOTES*

• *SEAFOOD*

• CRAB CAKES

*The wonderful blue crab of Maryland is one of the most delectable foods
I know. There is no better way to eat it than in crab cakes.*

*Recipes are intensely personal, with debate centering on seasoning and the
amount of bread crumbs added to help bind the crab cakes together. Too
much bread is disdained as filler.*

*Here's my recipe, which uses only one slice of bread. The crab cakes are pan
fried, rather than deep fried, which is traditional.*

*I prefer to let the taste of crab dominate and forego such additions as onion
or bell peppers or spicy seasonings. Only lump crabmeat that has dime and
nickle-sized morsels of perfectly white crab will do.*

Makes 2 to 4 servings

1 pound lump crabmeat, fresh or pasteurized	1 teaspoon dry mustard
	3/4 teaspoon salt
1 slice bread, crusts trimmed*	1/4 teaspoon freshly ground black pepper
1 egg	
4 tablespoons mayonnaise	oil
1 tablespoon minced parsley	butter

Pick over the crabmeat carefully to remove any bits of cartilage. Be gentle -
you're paying dearly for those lumps of crab. Set aside.

Cube the bread and run through a food processor to make rough crumbs. Blend
egg, mayonnaise, parsley and seasonings, and add the bread crumbs. Gently blend
in crab. Shape into four patties about an inch thick.

In a skillet heat equal parts of oil and butter to cover the pan about 1/4 inch
deep. Fry the patties for about 3 to 4 minutes per side, until nicely browned.
Alternatively broil under a preheated broiler about 3 minutes a side.

*Or use 1/4 cup cracker crumbs.

NOTE: For added flavor, add 1 teaspoon Worcestershire sauce or 1 teaspoon Old
Bay Seasoning to the mix.

• CHESAPEAKE BAY STEAMED SHRIMP

Here is an all-American recipe for spicy, peel-and-eat Chesapeake Bay steamed shrimp, using the Old Bay seasoning more usually used in cooking the blue crabs from those waters. They are finger-licking good. Serve as an appetizer or as a main course.

Makes 2 to 4 servings

1 pound large shrimp
water
distilled vinegar
2 tablespoons Old Bay seafood seasoning
1 teaspoon kosher salt

Fill the pot to be used for steaming to a depth of at least 1 inch with a mixture of 4 parts water to 1 part vinegar.

Combine the seasoning mixture and salt.

Layer the shrimp in a steamer basket, sprinkling each layer heavily with the seasoning mix. Bring the water to a boil, cover and steam until the shrimp is opaque throughout, about 3 to 5 minutes, depending on size.

Serve with beer.

• TIP

Most home cooks — and most restaurants — overcook shrimp. They should be moist and tender; not firm. Generally, the so-called large shrimp, which are actually on the small size, cook in no more than 3 minutes.

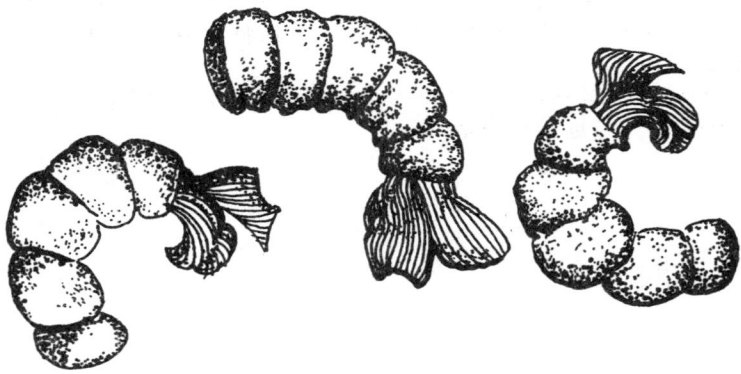

• LINDA'S MAXIMUM-FLAVOR SHRIMP

A food editors conference is much like any other professional conference. We listen to speakers, go to workshops — and eat. The difference is, we probably eat more and we never stop talking about food.

So it was one year in New Orleans. One night I sat across the table from Linda Cicero from the "Miami Herald." She believes that people in this country who say they love shrimp actually like the cocktail sauce on the cold shrimp or the garlic on the scampi.

Florida may be shrimp headquarters in this country, but in a moment of heresy she confided that shrimp, compared to lobster and crab, has little flavor. So she shared a secret for maximizing the flavor of shrimp.

It's the technique that counts here. Skip the usual water or beer. These shrimp cook only in their own juices.

Makes 2 servings

1 pound large raw shrimp (in the shell)
1 teaspoon salt
1/8 teaspoon cayenne pepper

Since we don't get fresh shrimp here, you'll have to settle for thawed frozen shrimp.

Dump the shrimp into a 12-inch pot that has a tight cover. Do not rinse the shrimp. Do not shell them. If the shrimp seem very dry, splash a little water in the pot.

Mix the salt and cayenne pepper and sprinkle over the shrimp. Cover the pot, light the fire, turn it to high. Put the pot over the heat and start counting. After 2 minutes, stir the shrimp, cover quickly and cook another minute or two, depending on the size of the shrimp. To check doneness, cut one in half to see that it's opaque throughout.

Quickly dump the shrimp on a plate. Sit down and start peeling. Dip shrimp in butter with a little lemon juice.

• GINGERED SCALLOPS

One of the attractions—and there are many—of Oriental-style cooking is the speed with which so many dishes are prepared.

The stir-fry technique, using small pieces of quick-cooking seafood or chicken, results in main courses that can be cooked in less than 5 minutes.

Sometimes there's additional time to be spent in chopping and dicing other ingredients, but in this recipe for gingered scallops, preparation can also be kept to under 5 minutes.

Bay scallops are ideal; if using sea scallops, cut them in half horizontally.

Makes 4 servings

1 ¹/₂ pounds fresh scallops
3 green onions, including tops
4 tablespoons peanut oil
2 teaspoons finely minced
ginger root*

1 large clove garlic, minced
1 teaspoon salt
freshly ground black pepper

Pat scallops dry on paper towels. Chop the green onions.

Put skillet over high heat; when hot, add the oil and swirl in the pan. Add the scallops, ginger and garlic and stir fry no more than 2 minutes. Add the salt, pepper and green onions and stir just until onions get limp. Serve with rice.

You can give the scallops a Szechuan taste if you add half a dried red pepper, seeds removed, to the oil along with the scallops.

*Do not substitute ground ginger for the fresh ginger root.

• ORIENTAL TUNA STEAKS

Fresh tuna, which takes wonderfully to grilling, looks more like beefsteak than fish. It lightens considerably when cooked, but there still is a meaty resemblance to steak.

One of the most fashionable ways to serve fresh tuna is to cook it medium rare, slice it and fan the slices on a plate. Fresh tuna prepared this way is a signature dish at stylish restaurants in major cities, and the presentation stretches an expensive piece of fish.

A Jackie's in Chicago, chef Jackie Etcheber marinates the tuna in soy and sesame sauce.

Here's my adaptation of Jackie's tuna steaks. You can cook the fish fully, but it won't be the same. Be careful not to overcook tuna, for it has a tendency to be dry.

Makes 4 servings

1 pound tuna steaks, cut 1-inch thick	1/2 teaspoon sesame oil
2 tablespoons soy sauce	1 clove garlic, crushed
1 tablespoon white wine	1/4 teaspoon grated ginger

Put the tuna in a glass baking dish and add the remaining ingredients. Marinate 1 hour at room temperature or in the refrigerator for 2 hours.

Prepare the fire in a covered grill, using hickory charcoal. Brush grill with oil so fish doesn't stick.

Cook on a slow fire for 7 to 10 minutes. (While you can sear the tuna on a hot fire, I've found I have better control with a slow fire.) Cut into fish to check doneness. It should still be red in the center.

To serve, slice across the grain into quarter-inch strips. Fan out on each plate.

Serve alongside a salad of red leaf lettuce and curly endive sprinkled with toasted sesame seeds.

• ORIENTAL STEAMED FISH

When the recipe instructions call for steaming fish or chicken, most people turn the page. They don't have a steamer. But it's easy to improvise one and the result is moist and tender.

To steam fish, put seasoned steaks or fillets skin-side down on a plate that will fit in a large pot. Make sure there's space around the edge of the plate so you can lift the plate out later.

Put an empty tuna can or custard cup in the pot, add an inch of water and rest the plate on the can. Cover and steam.

Here's an Oriental version I like.

Makes 4 servings

2 tablespoons light soy sauce
1 teaspoon sugar
1/4 cup peanut oil
1 teaspoon Oriental sesame oil

2 cloves garlic, peeled
1 ¹/₂ pounds fish steaks or fillets*
4 green onions, chopped
4 thin slices ginger, shredded

Mix soy sauce and sugar; set aside.

Heat oils, add garlic, cooking until the garlic turns light brown. Discard garlic and set aside. Put fish on an oven-proof plate and sprinkle with green onions. Put plate on top of an empty can in a large pot with an inch of water in the bottom.

Cover, bring to a boil and steam for 10 minutes per inch of thickness of fish. When done, drain off accumulated juices; pour soy mix over.

Reheat oil and add ginger, cooking until light brown. Pour over the fish. It will sizzle.

*Use a mild white fish that is fresh not frozen for this dish. Walleye is a good choice.

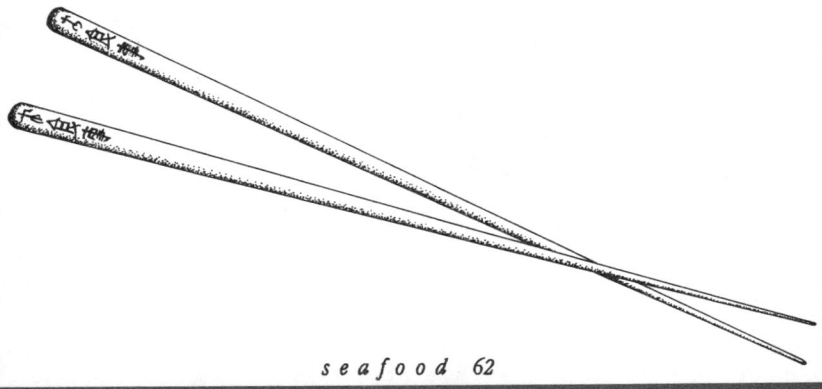

• GOLDEN WALLEYE

This recipe is a makeover of one I used to fix regularly in which a mixture of mayonnaise and mustard was slathered on fish fillets and run under the broiler. The result tasted a lot like fish with hollandaise sauce.

This version cuts the fat considerably by mixing a little mayo with non-fat yogurt. But it remains as one of those favorite 10-minute recipes.

The topping is good paired with mild white fish such as walleye.

Makes 2 servings

4 teaspoons non-fat yogurt
2 teaspoons mayonnaise
1 teaspoon Dijon mustard
salt and freshly ground
   black pepper

2 (6 to 8-ounce) walleye fillets
2 tablespoons dry white wine
cayenne pepper, optional
fresh minced parsley

Blend the yogurt, mayonnaise and mustard in a small bowl and set aside.

Sprinkle the fillets with salt and pepper and place, skin-side down, in a shallow, oven-proof pan such as a gratin dish. Sprinkle the wine over the fish.

Preheat the oven broiler and cook the fish, about 5 inches from the heat for 4 to 5 minutes.

Remove from the oven and spread the yogurt mixture over the fish. Sprinkle lightly with cayenne pepper.

Run the fish under the broiler for 3 to 5 minutes until the topping bubbles and browns. The fish should be opaque throughout. Sprinkle with minced parsley before serving.

• GRILLED LEMON SWORDFISH

Bay leaves are so basic that people who don't have much else in the way of spices may have an aging jar on the shelf. They seem to last forever because most cooks only use them in a soup or stew.

I like to keep a small plant growing in the house so I can use fresh bay leaves the way some Mediterranean cooks do. In Sicily, cooks skewer pieces of swordfish with the bay leaves in between, then grill them. Here's an easy workday adaptation using dried bay leaves. The fish marinates only as long as it takes to get the grill going.

Makes 2 to 3 servings

12 dried bay leaves
1 pound swordfish, cut at least 1-inch thick
1 lemon
2 tablespoons olive oil
1 clove garlic, crushed
salt and pepper

Pour boiling water over the bay leaves and let them soak. Soak 4 to 6 wooden skewers at the same time.

Cut the swordfish into 1- by 1 $\frac{1}{2}$-inch pieces. Juice the lemon and mix with the oil. Use a zester or grater to zest one half the lemon and add that to the mixture. Add the garlic, salt and pepper to taste and pour the mixture over the swordfish cubes, tossing to coat with the mixture.

Start the fire in the grill and let fish marinate until coals are ready.

Thread the fish on the skewers, alternating with the bay leaves. Grill, turning once, for 8 to 10 minutes.

NOTE: Do not let the fish marinate longer than 1 hour or it can become mushy.

• GARLIC SAUTEED FISH

Some people make it look really simple.
They work away from home all day and still come home and put an appeal-ing meal on the table in less than an hour.
What's more, they scorn convenience foods and cook everything from scratch.
The secret? Well, there are many. And one is serving chicken and fish fre-quently. They both cook quickly and can be varied in infinite fashion.
This fish dish is robust with flavor, and it couldn't be quicker. It's a family favorite served by my sister.

Makes 4 to 6 servings

1 ½ pounds fish fillets	1/4 cup minced fresh parsley
salt and pepper to taste	1 clove garlic, minced
2 tablespoons butter	3 tablespoons lemon juice
1 tablespoon vegetable oil	

Sprinkle fish with salt and pepper. Melt butter with oil and heat. Saute the fish for about 5 minutes, turning once. Sprinkle parsley, garlic and lemon juice over fish and cook over low heat for 3 to 5 minutes.

Serve the fish with a tossed green salad and rice and you can have dinner on the table in half an hour. Just remember to start the rice first.

• TIP

To prevent fillets from curling when pan frying, use a sharp knife to lightly score the skin.

• POTATOES,
  RICE & BEANS

• FOOL-THE-EYE MASHED POTATOES

Buttery rich mashed potatoes are the essence of comfort food, but great quantities of butter make me nervous these days.

Now I'm not about to mash potatoes with water and resort to Butter Buds. I still want the real thing, so enter the world of illusion.

These mashed potatoes look buttery rich because they are made with yellow potatoes, either Yukon Gold or Finnish. They're cooked with garlic to add a flavor boost, but you could use onion. They're whipped with buttermilk, which is lower in butterfat than cream, but rich-tasting.

And the topping of one single pat of butter – about a tablespoon – melting down the sides of a mountain of buttery-yellow potatoes fools the eye – and maybe the palate.

So eat them and feel virtuous. Remember that James Beard added 6 tablespoons butter and a half cup of cream to the same amount of potatoes.

Makes 6 servings

6 medium Yukon Gold or Finnish potatoes	1/2 cup buttermilk
1 to 2 cloves garlic, peeled	freshly ground white pepper
salt	1 tablespoon butter

Peel the potatoes and cut into halves or quarters. Place in a medium saucepan with cold water to cover and add the garlic and sprinkle with salt. Cover and cook until just tender. Drain off potato water and place potatoes over warm heat to dry off excess moisture. Remove garlic cloves if desired but it's not necessary; they mash easily with the potatoes.

Meanwhile, warm the buttermilk slightly. Using a potato masher or electric beater, mash the potatoes and beat in the buttermilk. Season generously with salt and pepper. Pile the potatoes into a serving dish and top with the butter.

If desired, mix in fresh snipped chives for added color and flavor.

• GARLIC ROASTED POTATOES

*I could make a meal out of a plate of fresh buttered asparagus, but potatoes?
You bet, when they're these potatoes.*

The recipe comes from Alice Waters, via the Potato Board. Waters is the chef-owner of Chez Panisse in Berkley, Calif., and is close enough to Gilroy, the garlic capital of the world, to make good use of that native crop.

Whole unpeeled cloves of garlic are roasted with the potatoes. Each diner squeezes some of the sweet, mild roasted garlic on the potatoes.

It is not a dish for those who don't appreciate garlic, and certainly not for those who are too fastidious to get their hands dirty. But for those who like to dig into great flavor, it's a wonderful, incredibly easy side dish, or meal.

Makes 6 servings

12 medium new potatoes, or
    Finnish potatoes, unpeeled
1 ¹⁄₂ heads fresh garlic

coarse sea salt
coarse ground black pepper
olive oil

Wash the potatoes and dry. Cut into quarters. Separate the garlic into individual cloves but do not peel.

Arrange the potatoes skin-side down in a lightly oiled baking dish that will just hold them. Scatter the cloves of garlic over the top. Sprinkle generously with salt and pepper and drizzle olive oil over the top.

Cook in a preheated 325-degree oven for 50 to 60 minutes, stirring once to coat with the oil. The potatoes should be just tender when pricked with a fork.

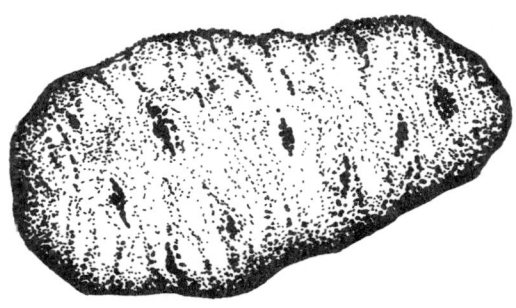

• NEW POTATOES WITH GREMOLADA

We get a double harvest of little potatoes. In the spring, the new potatoes arrive at the supermarket from "away." Then, in the fall, local farmers dig their potatoes and set out baskets of tiny ones harvested with the crop.

Using the tiny, thin-skinned potatoes is a real time-saver, for they don't have to be peeled, just scrubbed. In this recipe, the potatoes are steamed, tossed with olive oil and sprinkled with a mixture of lemon peel, parsley and garlic that the Italians call gremolada. It's traditionally sprinkled on osso buco alla Milanese, but it works well on meatless dishes, too.

Makes 4 to 6 servings

2 pounds new potatoes*
1 ¹/₂ tablespoons finely chopped garlic
1 ¹/₂ tablespoons
     finely chopped lemon peel
1/2 cup finely chopped parsley

2 tablespoons olive oil
1/2 teaspoon salt
1/4 teaspoon freshly ground
     black pepper

Scrub the potatoes and steam them until they are just tender – if they are small and fresh, they may cook in as little as 10 minutes. Larger potatoes may take 20 minutes.

While they cook, prepare the gremolada. Combine the garlic, lemon peel and parsley on a cutting board and chop to combine them.

Put the olive oil in a 10-inch skillet over medium high heat. Add the steamed potatoes and sprinkle them with salt and pepper. Toss them with a wooden spoon until the potatoes are evenly coated with oil. Remove the skillet from the heat and toss the potatoes with the gremolada. Serve immediately in a heated serving dish.

*For even cooking, the potatoes should be the same size.

• COCONUT RICE

Rice is the staple of the Orient. When you eat the Thai way, you have a large serving of rice and take morsels of the accompanying dishes, which are all served at the same time.

Usually the rice is plain, but at banquets it gets special treatment. Pineapple fried rice, served in a hollowed-out pineapple, is one specialty. Coconut rice is another.

When we sampled it at one brunch banquet in Singapore, the coconut rice was served with an array of condiments to sprinkle on top as desired.

I use a three-piece rice steamer, and steam the rice, covered, for 25 minutes, but you can prepare it without a steamer.

Makes 6 servings

1 cup chicken stock	2 tablespoons fried
1/2 cup unsweetened coconut milk*	shallots or garlic*
1 cup Thai fragrant rice*	1/4 cup redskin peanuts
1 teaspoon salt	chopped green onion tops

Combine the stock and coconut milk in a heavy-bottomed saucepan and heat. Add the rice and salt, and bring to a boil. Boil for 1 minute, then turn the heat down, cover and cook undisturbed for 18 minutes. Remove from heat and let sit for at least 10 minutes. It can sit for up to 30 minutes.

Fluff the rice with a fork and mound in a serving dish – traditionally a flat woven basket – and sprinkle with the fried shallots, peanuts and onion tops.

* Look for fragrant rice, coconut milk and jars of fried onions at Oriental food stores. Imported rice should be washed in running water until it runs clear. Do not use coconut cream that is sold for drinks.

NOTE: Optional condiments to sprinkle over rice include minced chilies and chopped cilantro.

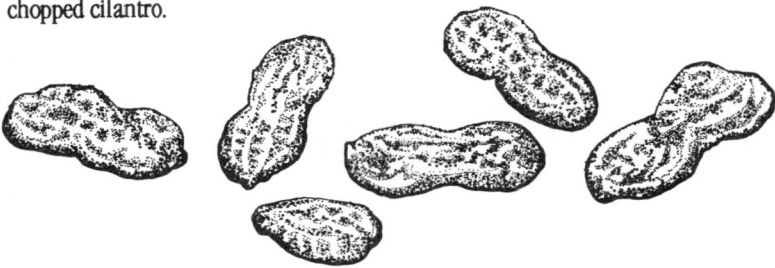

• CURRIED BASMATI RICE

We all prepare some favorite dishes for a while, then relegate the recipe to the file box. So, while I was enamored of basmati rice, the aromatic rice from India, I eventually ran out and forgot about it.

Then the trade people from the Rice Council stopped by, pushing the U.S.-grown Texmati rice. Well, I tried that, and while it's nice to buy American when we can, something's missing from the home-grown variety. What's missing is basmati's flowery aroma that makes the kitchen smell so good.

So I went back to the Indian rice and rediscovered the pleasures in this recipe.

Makes 4 servings

2 tablespoons olive or peanut oil
1/2 cup minced sweet onion
   (Walla Walla, Vidalia or Maui)
1 large clove garlic, minced
1/2 teaspoon curry powder
1/2 red bell pepper, minced
1 3/4 cups chicken broth
salt
1 cup basmati rice

Heat the oil over medium heat in a pan with a tight-fitting lid. Saute the onion and garlic for 2 to 3 minutes, but don't let the garlic brown. Stir in the curry powder and mix well.

Add the red pepper and saute for several minutes. Add the chicken broth and salt to taste. (With homemade stock you may use 1/2 teaspoon, but use less with salty, canned stock.)

Bring to a boil, add the rice and stir. Cover, turn the heat down to maintain just a simmer. Cook for about 15 minutes.

When all the liquid has been absorbed, remove cover and place a paper towel over the pot. Replace lid and let the rice rest for 5 to 10 minutes. This technique, passed on by an Indian friend, produces a drier, fluffier rice. Stir before serving.

* For a more authentic flavor, add 1 teaspoon toasted cumin seed with the curry.

• LEMON RICE WITH PINE NUTS

Whenever a recipe in the paper calls for lemon zest, an editor comes running with the question: What's lemon zest?

Zest means something different to non cooks, though the first definition in Webster's big dictionary makes it clear that it's part of the fruit.

To make it simple: everyone knows what lemon peel is. If you peel too deeply, you get into the white pith, which is bitter. If you peel lightly, what you have is the zest of the lemon (or orange or lime) – the thin, outer skin. It's the flavorful part.

The best way to separate it from the fruit is with a lemon zester; a gadget that's a great stocking stuffer. It strips the zest off in strands.

It's lemon zest that adds the zing to this recipe for rice with pine nuts.

Makes 4 servings

2 tablespoons butter	1 teaspoon lemon zest
1/2 cup chopped onion	1/2 cup toasted pine nuts
1 cup long-grain rice	1/4 cup fresh herbs
1 $1/_2$ cups hot chicken broth	

Melt the butter in a heavy-bottomed saucepan. Add the onion and cook until softened, but not brown. Add the rice and stir to coat with the butter. Cook over medium heat, stirring, about 5 minutes.

Stir in the chicken broth and lemon zest and cover. When the broth returns to boil, reduce the heat and cook 17 minutes. There should be no liquid remaining.

Stir in the pine nuts and cover the pot with a double thickness of paper towels, Replace cover and set the pot aside for 10 minutes.

Just before serving, stir in the herbs. Use easily available herbs such as parsley or chives, or a pinch of green onion tops.

• TIPSY RICE

Years ago, in this column, I ran a recipe for baked rice. It's a foolproof recipe for cooking rice. Using this technique, the rice never scorches or sticks to the bottom of the pan and the grains are always perfectly cooked.

Over the years I have varied the recipe. I use less oil and a little less salt now. Recently I decided to use up a bit of wine in the refrigerator and substituted it for part of the water in the recipe. It added a wonderful flavor.

A dry chardonnay or a flowery sauvignon blanc is fine. Don't use that stuff sold as cooking wine that just tastes salty.

Here's my '90s version of baked rice. I call it tipsy rice – but most of the alcohol cooks off.

Makes 4 servings

1 tablespoon olive oil
4 green onions
1 cup rice
3/4 teaspoon salt

freshly ground black pepper*
1/2 cup white wine
1 cup water

Preheat oven to 400 degrees. Heat the oil in a heavy-bottomed pan that has a tight-fitting lid (foil can be used). Add the green onion and rice and stir to coat the grains with oil. Saute for several minutes over medium heat but do not let the rice or onion brown.

Sprinkle with salt and pepper to taste. Add the wine and water and return to a boil. Cover and bake for 17 minutes. Remove from oven Remove cover and place a double thickness of paper towels over the top. Replace cover and let stand 10 minutes. Fluff with a fork before serving.

*Or add a dried red chili pepper for added flavor.

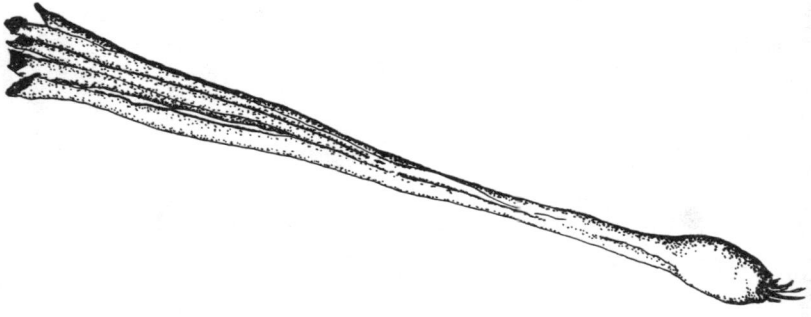

• WILD WILD RICE

One of my Christmas presents always is a supply of wild rice from a friend whose family lives in Minnesota. It is enough to carry me through Easter and then some.

There is something about wild rice that connotes celebrations, and it's not just the price. It is exotic.

When I first returned the favor, preparing the rice for my friend, he had the ultimate compliment. He wanted the recipe for his Minnesota mom. My way was best, he said.

I added excitement to the rice with both dried wild mushrooms and pecans. The mushrooms are optional.

Makes 4 servings

1 cup wild rice
3 cups water
1 teaspoon salt
1 to 2 ounces dried mushrooms*

3 tablespoons chopped pecans
1 $\frac{1}{2}$ tablespoons butter
freshly grated nutmeg

Rinse the rice under cold water until the water runs clear. Drain. Bring 3 cups water to a boil and add rice and salt. Cover and simmer over low heat for 35 to 45 minutes, until the water is evaporated and the rice is cooked. Do not overcook to the mushy stage.

While rice cooks, soak dried mushrooms in warm water for 30 minutes. Dice mushrooms, discarding the hard stems. Saute the mushroom pieces and pecans in the butter.

When rice is done, remove from heat, cover with a paper towel, replace lid and let stand off the heat for 10 minutes. Just before serving, stir in the pecans and mushrooms and a few gratings of nutmeg.

* European mushrooms such as porcini or chanterelles are preferred to Oriental mushrooms for this recipe. Since they are expensive, the amount used depends on your pocketbook. Soak them ahead of time and you can include the flavorful strained liquid in the water to cook the rice.

• WILD RICE PANCAKES

We are creatures of the seasons. So as the sharp winds tug at the brightly colored leaves, the foods that sound appealing are as different from summer as the temperature.

Fall is the time for game, at least for those who have hunters in the family or who go to the restaurants that feature it. Whenever I think of game, I also think of wild rice – a standard accompaniment.

This recipe for a wild rice pancake is a savory side dish.

Makes 6 servings

1 cup salted water	1 cup (5 ounces) blanched almonds, toasted
1/3 cup rinsed wild rice	1 cup flour
2 tablespoons butter	1/4 cup minced green onion, including tops
2 cups milk	pinch cream of tartar
1 teaspoon salt	vegetable oil and butter
4 eggs, separated	

Bring water to a boil; add rice, cover and simmer 45 minutes until tender. Drain and set aside.

Melt the butter and cool it; combine butter with the milk and salt and add to the drained rice. Beat the egg yolks for 3 minutes, then combine with rice. Stir in the nuts, flour and green onion.

Beat the egg whites and cream of tartar until stiff. Fold into the rice batter. Heat 1 tablespoon each of oil and butter in a skillet over medium heat. Ladle 2 $\frac{1}{2}$-inch pancakes into the skillet. Cook until the bottom is golden brown, flip and brown other side. Repeat with remaining batter, adding more oil and butter as needed. Keep pancakes warm on a platter in a 175-degree oven.

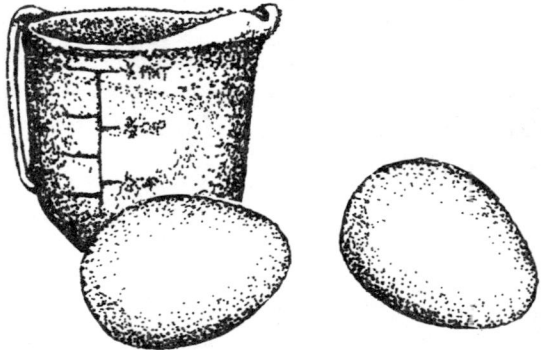

• DRUNKEN BLACK BEANS

In recent years American cooks have added black beans to a kitchen larder that used to focus on navy beans and kidney beans. Credit that to increasing interest in the foods of Mexico, where black beans are a staple.

On one of my annual trips to Mexico, this one to Oaxaca, Chiapas and the Yucatan, black beans turned up on every plate, from breakfast to dinner. In an effort to duplicate one of the memories, I cooked this recipe. They are best made ahead.

These will be slightly soupy and are good served over rice. Or, raise the temperature, cook off the excess liquid, and serve the beans as fork food. They're delicious scooped up with warm flour tortillas.

Makes 8 servings

8 ounces dried black beans
6 cups water
4 tablespoons vegetable or olive oil
2 cloves garlic, peeled
1 large onion
1/2 tablespoon salt

1 cup tomatoes,
   drained and chopped
2 jalapeno peppers, minced
3/4 cup chopped cilantro
1 cup flat beer

Rinse the beans. Do not pre-soak. Put beans in a large pot with the water, 1 tablespoon of the oil, garlic and 1/2 the onion. Cover tightly, bring to a boil, reduce to a simmer and cook for 1 $\frac{1}{2}$ hours.

To test for doneness, remove a few beans with a wooden spoon and blow on them. If the skins split, they are done. Add the salt and cook another 30 minutes.

Chop the remaining half onion. In the remaining 3 tablespoons oil, saute the onion until soft. Add the tomatoes, minced jalapenos, 1/2 cup of the cilantro, the beans and beer. Simmer, uncovered for 45 minutes. Just before serving, add the remaining 1/4 cup cilantro.

NOTE: Never add salt in the beginning when cooking beans, or they will be tough.

- *NOTES*

• *VEGETABLES*

• BRAISED BABY ARTICHOKES

In the spring, for a brief time, baby artichokes show up at the supermarket and I always try to make this dish at least once.

The advantage of these miniatures is that there's no choke to worry about. It hasn't developed. Still the babies, which are no larger than a lemon and usually much smaller, must be trimmed so that they're entirely edible. Start snapping off the outer dark green leaves. Don't stop until you reach the pale, green inner leaves. You can cook the tiniest ones whole; cut others in half and drop into water with a little lemon juice until ready to cook.

Here's the best way I've found to cook them. They can be served as a side dish, but I love them tossed with pasta.

Makes 4 servings as a side dish, 2 main dish servings with pasta

6 baby artichokes	1 teaspoon dried oregano
2 tablespoons each butter	1 bay leaf
and olive oil	1/4 cup dry white wine
salt and pepper	1/2 to 3/4 cup chicken broth
2 garlic cloves, sliced	

Trim the artichokes, snapping off the dark outer leaves. Cut each artichoke into halves or quarters. Melt the butter with oil in a non-aluminum skillet. Add the artichokes and garlic; saute over medium heat until the artichokes begin to color. Sprinkle with salt and pepper. Add the oregano, bay leaf and wine; cover and cook over medium heat. As the liquid cooks off, add 1/4 cup chicken broth, cover and continue cooking, adding more stock as necessary, until artichokes are just tender

• TIP

Recipes sometimes specify using a "non-reactive" skillet or saucepan. That rules out aluminum or cast iron pans, which interact with foods such as wine, tomatoes and artichokes, causing discoloring. Use stainless steel or enamel coated pans for such dishes.

• DOUBLE SESAME ASPARAGUS

Though I've modified my cooking habits over the years, I'll never give up butter on some things. Corn on the cob without butter? Never. Asparagus without butter? Not likely, I've always said.

But I've discovered an alternative, at least for asparagus. The Oriental touch of sesame oil, barely a dribble of the stuff, infuses the vegetable with flavor. The addition of chicken broth, cooked down to a glaze, helps coat each spear.

This recipe uses both sesame oil and a sprinkling of toasted seeds.

Makes 4 servings

1 pound asparagus	1 teaspoon Oriental sesame oil
1/2 teaspoon salt	freshly ground black pepper
2 tablespoons reduced-salt chicken broth	2 tablespoons toasted sesame seed

Trim the asparagus, either snapping the spears where they break naturally – the easiest way – or cutting them into uniform lengths and peeling the tough ends.

Bring a large skillet full of water to a boil and add the salt. Cook the asparagus, uncovered until it is just tender-crisp when pricked with a fork. Timing depends largely on how fresh the asparagus is. Drain the asparagus and rinse under cold water to stop the cooking. Set aside.

When ready to serve, put the chicken broth, sesame oil and asparagus in the skillet and heat over high heat, shaking skillet so the spears become glazed with the oil and broth mixture. Sprinkle with pepper and sesame seeds before serving.

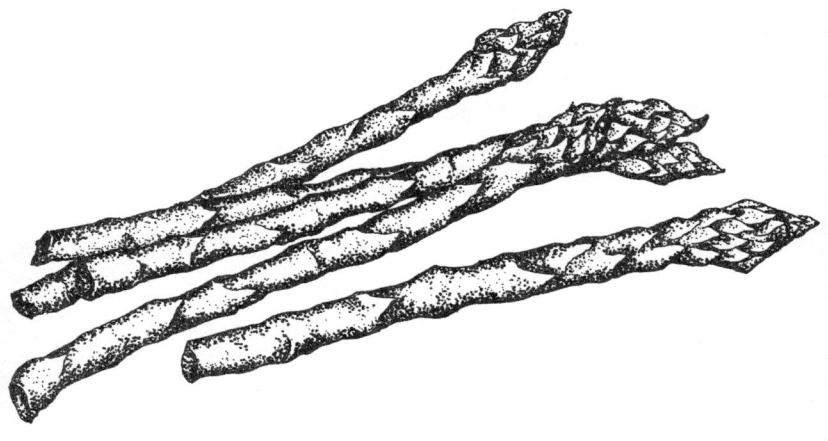

• ASPARAGUS WITH ORANGE
  PECAN BUTTER

I have more recipes for asparagus than any other vegetable, so I'm sharing two in this book.

This recipe takes buttered asparagus two steps further. Orange peel and juice add a complex flavor. If that sounds unusual, remember that asparagus is frequently served with sauce Maltaise, an orange-flavored hollandaise, but this is much more simple to make. The addition of pecans adds texture, but can be optional.

When selecting asparagus, remember that smaller isn't always better in selecting vegetables. When it comes to asparagus, I find that thin spears are less tender and less flavorful than medium-sized stalks.

And be mindful that freshly picked asparagus cooks much faster than asparagus that has been sitting around.

Serves 8 to 10

3 pounds fresh snapped asparagus
1/4 cup butter
1/3 cup coarsely chopped pecans

1 teaspoon orange juice
1/2 teaspoon grated orange peel
2 teaspoons salt

Wash asparagus and pare ends of spears to ensure even cooking.

In a small pan, melt the butter and stir in pecans, orange juice and peel and set aside.

For 3 pounds of asparagus, use two large skillets, half full of water. Bring to a boil and add 1 teaspoon salt to each. Add asparagus and cover only until water returns to a boil. Cook just until a fork will pierce the asparagus. Drain and serve immediately, with orange pecan butter spooned over the asparagus.

• *BROCCOLI WITH GINGER SAUCE*

Broccoli may not be my favorite vegetable – asparagus is – but I use more broccoli than anything else.

The health benefits are attractive, but so is its versatility, as well as its usual modest price.

Because of its assertive flavor, broccoli can stand up to robust Oriental seasonings that are more healthful than the traditional butter.

Here's a variation that's good warm or cold. Because the sauce is uncooked, the ginger is crushed in a garlic press to extract its juice. You get the flavor without the fibrous bits of ginger.

Makes 6 servings

1/4 (scant) cup
   thick slices of fresh ginger
1 clove garlic
2 teaspoons lime juice
2 teaspoons soy sauce

1/2 teaspoon sugar
  pinch cayenne pepper
1 tablespoon Oriental sesame oil*
1 bunch broccoli

Press the chopped ginger in a garlic press to extract the juice. You should have about 1 1/4 teaspoons juice. Press the garlic through the garlic press and scrape into a small bowl.

Add the ginger juice, lime juice, soy sauce, sugar and pepper and blend well. Whisk in the sesame oil.

Wash the broccoli and break off flowerettes. Lightly peel the stalks and cut into 1/2-inch chunks. Cook in boiling, salted water until tender crisp, about 4 to 6 minutes depending on the size of the flowerettes. Drain and toss with 1 tablespoon vegetable oil. Drizzle with ginger dressing.

*Or use 2 teaspoons sesame oil plus 1 teaspoon chili oil.

• *CARROTS WITH CRANBERRIES*

If you're looking for something different to put on the Thanksgiving dinner table, I heartily suggest this side dish.

For this dish, carrots are cooked with a little cider and butter and given color and tartness with a cup of cranberries. It looks lovely on the table.

Put in a shallow casserole and you can slip it onto the bottom rack of the oven under the turkey.

Makes 6 servings

1 apple, grated
1 cup cranberries, washed
4 cups grated carrots*
4 tablespoons light brown sugar

1/2 teaspoon salt
1/2 cup apple cider
2 tablespoons butter

Combine the apple, cranberries, carrots, sugar, salt and cider. Place in a buttered casserole and dot with butter. Cover and bake in a preheated 350-degree oven for 40 minutes, stirring once.

*Instead of grating carrots, I slice them thinly in the food processor.

• DILLED CARROTS

*A carrot a day may replace an apple a day as a slice of nutritional guid-
ance to good health.*

*Our mothers always told us to eat carrots for our eyes. But contemporary
research shows that the beta-carotene in carrots and some other yellow and
dark-green vegetables and fruits may help protect against cancer.*

*I've tried to put carrots back on the menu, and I know no more flavorful
way than these dilled carrots. Fresh dill is available in the produce section in
some supermarkets and at farmers markets in summer. Do not substitute
dill seed.*

Makes 2 servings

6 medium carrots, pared
2 cups chicken broth (14 $\frac{1}{2}$-ounce can)
2 tablespoons fresh dill weed, snipped
freshly ground black pepper

Slice the carrots in half lengthwise. Place them in a skillet with the chicken broth,
which should almost cover the carrots. Do not cover skillet.

Bring the broth to a boil and simmer until the carrots are just tender and the
liquid has almost evaporated. The broth should just coat the carrots. Add the dill and
stir to coat the carrots with the herb. Sprinkle with pepper.

• GRILLED EGGPLANT

While most of my garden is devoted to flowers and herbs, I always tuck in some Japanese eggplant, which produce small, elongated purple fruit. With their pretty purple flowers, the plants are a form of edible landscaping.

These small meaty eggplants have few seeds and take well to grilling, a technique that doesn't require as much oil as is used in most eggplant recipes.

There's no point giving the amounts for such a recipe. Figure on one small eggplant per person.

Japanese eggplant
vegetable oil
lemon juice
pesto sauce, optional

Remove caps from eggplant, but do not peel. Slice lengthwise, about 1/2-inch thick. Sprinkle with salt and set in a colander for 30 minutes to drain. (While not all eggplant is bitter, this ensures that it won't be.) Scrape off any visible salt and pat eggplant slices dry with paper towels.

Make a basting sauce with two parts oil to one part lemon juice. When coals are covered with gray ash, brush eggplant with oil and lemon mixture. Grill, turning once until eggplant is brown on the cut side and can be easily pierced with a fork. This takes just a matter of minutes so don't leave the grill. Serve as is or with a little pesto sauce drizzled over the hot eggplant.

• TIP

Pesto sauce is available in supermarkets and gourmet food shops, but it's never as good as homemade. To make your own: Puree 2 cups basil leaves, 1/2 cup olive oil, 2 cloves garlic, 1 teaspoon salt and 2 tablespoons pine nuts in a blender.

With a spoon, mix in 1/2 cup grated Parmesan cheese and 2 tablespoons softened butter.

• STIR-FRIED KALE

I grew up eating greens such as kale and Swiss chard. The latter, used widely in Italy, seems never to be available in supermarkets here but is one of the best vegetables for the garden since it withstands cold better than nearly any crop. We sometimes had it on Thanksgiving, fresh from the garden.

Kale, on the other hand, is available, but it has been mostly misused by chain restaurants, which have used it as a silly, raw garnish.

While some people boil kale in the manner of classic "greens," I like it stir-fried until just tender and still bright green. Blanch it first to wilt the kale; that makes it easier to manage in the skillet or wok.

Makes 4 servings

1 pound kale
boiling water
2 tablespoons olive oil
2 cloves garlic, sliced thin

1/4 teaspoon salt
freshly ground black pepper
chicken broth

Wash the kale and trim out and discard the thick stalks. Tear leaves into pieces. Place in a colander and pour boiling water over kale to wilt the greens. Drain well and set aside.

Heat a large skillet and swirl in the oil; add the garlic slices, stir to coat with oil and immediately add the kale.

Stir fry, tossing to coat with oil. Sprinkle with the salt and pepper. Add a tablespoon or two of chicken broth if necessary to moisten the kale.

Cook, uncovered, only until the kale is just tender.

• MEXICAN CORN

On the streets of Mexico, vendors with pushcarts and makeshift stands sell corn on the cob. They also sell little cups filled with kernels cut from the cob, sprinkled with cilantro and served with half a "limon," the little lime that is ever-present there.

This recipe for corn cooked with hot pepper and cilantro borrows from that street food. It's an excellent side dish.

The amount of heat can be modified for your tastes. If you or your guests can't tolerate hot food, use the jalapeno peppers but remove the veins and the seeds.

Makes 4 servings

4 tablespoons butter	6 tablespoons cilantro, chopped
3/4 cup chopped onion	1/2 cup water
2 $\frac{1}{2}$ tablespoons minced	salt to taste
jalapeno pepper	additional cilantro, minced
4 cups frozen corn kernels	fresh lime, cut in half

Heat the butter in a medium-sized saucepan or skillet. Over medium heat, saute the onion and pepper until soft. Stir in the corn, 6 tablespoons cilantro, water and salt. Cover tightly and cook over low heat until the corn is tender. Stir occasionally so that it doesn't stick to the bottom of the pan.

Place in a serving dish and sprinkle with the additional cilantro. Serve with a bowl of cut limes to squeeze over the corn.

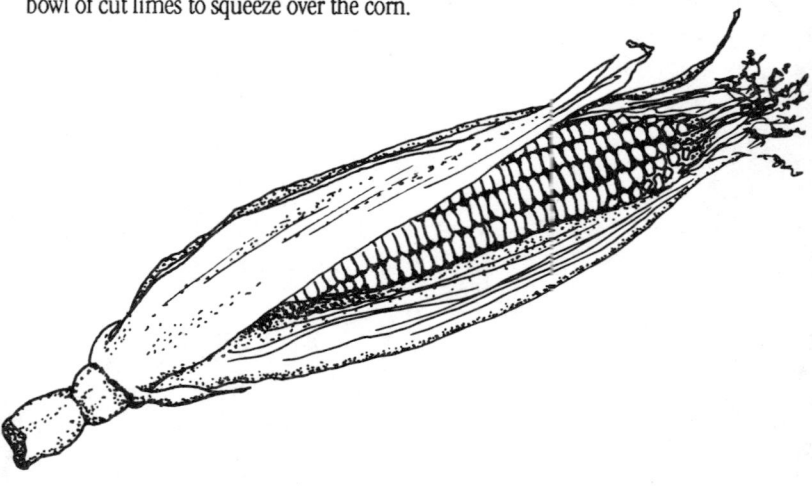

• RED BELL PEPPER SAUTE

I have never refused to share a recipe and am suspect of those who do. But I was tempted once.

The dish was an unusual, dramatic and intensely flavored saute of red bell peppers, flavored with, among other things, almonds, garlic, one anchovy and cilantro. I immediately passed the recipe to a friend who also loves cooking and eating.

After she tried it and loved it, she implored me not to publish the recipe.

"They'll leave out the anchovy," she said. "They won't use cilantro. You watch." She's probably right.

And if they're left out of the dish, of course it won't be the same. While the anchovy isn't identifiable, in combination with the other ingredients it adds body and substance to the sauce.

I printed the recipe anyway and continue to fix it regularly. It's good as a side dish and excellent served over pasta.

Makes 4 to 6 servings

1/2 cup chopped blanched almonds
1 tablespoon vegetable oil
2 red bell peppers, cut in
   1-inch squares
1 tablespoon sugar
1 teaspoon lemon juice

1 teaspoon salt
1/4 teaspoon red pepper flakes
1 clove garlic, chopped finely
1 anchovy, chopped finely
1 tablespoon finely chopped,
   fresh cilantro

Toast the almonds in a dry skillet for 10 minutes in a pre-heated 400 degree oven. Set aside. Heat oil in a skillet and saute bell peppers until just tender. Stir in sugar and cook, stirring constantly, until melted. Stir in lemon juice, salt, red pepper flakes, garlic, anchovy, cilantro and almonds.

• *SUGAR SNAP PEAS WITH WILD MUSHROOMS*

Sugar snap peas are the treasure of the late spring garden in southwest Ohio. Some people like to snack on them raw, but they're wonderful in quick stir-fries.

Knowing the affinity of peas for mushrooms, I came up with this recipe, using more flavorful "wild" mushrooms. Dried porcini or shiitake are the preferred choice, or use a quarter pound of fresh shiitake, sliced to be the same size as a snow pea. Sweet onions, such as Maui or Walla Walla sweets, add mellow flavor.

Makes 4 to 6 servings

1 ounce dried wild mushrooms,
   or 1/4 pound fresh shiitake
   mushrooms
1 pound sugar snap peas
1/2 sweet onion

1 tablespoon butter
1 tablespoon vegetable oil
1/2 teaspoon salt
 pinch sugar

Put the dried mushrooms in a small bowl and cover with hot water. Let the mushrooms soak for 30 minutes. Strain the mushrooms through a filter-lined strainer, reserving the liquid. Rinse the mushrooms well in cold water to remove any grit. Slice the mushrooms, discarding the stem, which is tough; place on paper towels to dry.

If using fresh mushrooms, wipe clean with a damp paper towel and slice, discarding the stem. Rinse the peas and remove the strings. Set aside to dry.

Put the onion cut side down on a cutting board and slice vertically.

Heat the butter and oil in a large skillet. Saute the onion and mushrooms until the onions are just tender. Add the peas and sprinkle with salt and sugar. Stir fry, tossing for 3 to 4 minutes. Add a little of the mushroom liquid to moisten the peas and steam for several minutes.

• ITALIAN TOMATOES

A favorite dish of mine combines parsley, toasted pine nuts, garlic and butter as a stuffing for lightly sauteed tomatoes.

This side dish is a far better accompaniment to meats than the ubiquitous crumb-topped baked tomato halves served at so many "better" restaurants. And the red, white and green color matches the Italian flag; hence their name.

Makes 6 servings

6 medium ripe tomatoes	1 cup minced parsley
1/2 cup pine nuts	3 cloves garlic, minced
1 stick butter	4 tablespoons olive oil

Cut the tomatoes in half; use a spoon to scoop out seeds. Sprinkle cut sides with salt and let drain on paper towels for 30 minutes. Toast the pine nuts in a small dry skillet in a 350 degree oven for 10 minutes. They should be light brown. Set aside.

In the same skillet, melt the butter and saute the garlic and parsley over moderate heat for 5 minutes. Meanwhile, saute the tomatoes, cut side down in the olive oil, for just 2 or 3 minutes until slightly softened. Spoon the parsley mixture into the tomatoes and top with pine nuts. Serve while warm, two per person.

• ZUCCHINI ON THE GRILL

All the French chefs and their sauces sometimes can't improve on natures' bounty. Take, for example, zucchini.

Whole cookbooks have been dedicated to the subject of the prolific vegetable. I realize that boredom has prompted most of the innovation, but this is one subject where less is more.

The delicate flavor shows best when little zucchini are just steamed until crisp and served with butter and fresh herbs, or sliced and sauteed with sweet onions.

But my favorite recipe is zucchini on the grill. It is utterly simple and the flavor is fabulous. They're good as is or enhanced with the flavor of smoke from hardwood chips. Fixed this way, they're very low in fat and calories.

Makes 4 servings

4 medium zucchini, 6 inches long
salt
safflower or olive oil
freshly ground black pepper

Slice the zucchini in half lengthwise. Sprinkle with salt and let stand in colander to draw out excess water. After 30 minutes, wipe off moisture with a paper towel.

Brush the squash on both sides with a little oil and sprinkle with pepper.

Place the squash cut-side down on an oiled grill, over a medium-hot fire. Cook for 4 to 5 minutes; the bottom should be very brown. Turn and cook just until a skewer easily pierces the squash.

Serve with added salt if desired.

NOTE: I add several handfuls of dampened grapevine cuttings to the fire when I cook zucchini. For added flavor, make a batch of basil or cilantro pesto (see index) and spread over grilled zucchini.

• *SALADS*

• CABBAGE SALAD WITH BLUE CHEESE

When the temperature drops, so does interest in salads, at least the traditional mixed green salad. But appetites can be revived by serving hearty robust salads with lots of texture.

This recipe was passed on by a friend one year. No little leaf lettuce salad this one. It's a real winter salad, packed with crunch and flavor.

And, if you've never eaten raw Brussels sprouts, their cabbage-like flavor is milder than when they're cooked.

Makes 16 servings

1 medium head red cabbage, coarsely shredded
1 box raw Brussels sprouts, washed, trimmed and sliced very thin
1/2 cup diced onion or chopped green onion
1/2 cup red wine vinegar
2 tablespoons Dijon mustard
1 teaspoon salt
1 teaspoon pepper
1 teaspoon sugar
3/4 cup olive oil
1 $\frac{1}{3}$ cups crumbled blue cheese

Mix the shredded cabbage, Brussels sprouts slices and onion. Whisk together vinegar, mustard, salt, pepper and sugar and blend in the oil. Toss the vegetables with the dressing. Just before serving, sprinkle with blue cheese.

NOTE: This salad can be easily cut in half or quartered.

• *MOROCCAN CARROT SALAD*

*When we were growing up, the school cafeteria lunches always included a
carrot salad. It was a sweet concoction made with raisins and Miracle Whip
salad dressing. Even as a kid, I viewed it as health food gone awry.*

*A more contemporary salad is this Moroccan carrot salad. The key
ingredient is the fresh lemon juice – please don't use bottled – and the
cumin seeds, which are more aromatic when freshly toasted and ground. If
you use bottled ground cumin, start with a half-teaspoon.*

Makes 4 servings

1 pound carrots
pinch of sugar
1 teaspoon cumin seeds
3 tablespoons fresh lemon juice
1/4 teaspoon salt
1/4 teaspoon freshly
    ground black pepper

1 tablespoon mild olive oil
1 clove garlic, minced
1/4 cup minced green onions
2 tablespoons minced
    fresh parsley

Peel carrots and cut on the diagonal to make large slices. Place in a saucepan
and cover with water. Add the sugar, cover and cook until just tender. Drain and
refresh under cold water.

Toast the cumin seeds in a small dry skillet for a minute or two until the
aroma rises. Grind the seeds in a mini-processor or crush with a heavy skillet.

Combine the lemon juice, salt, pepper, olive oil and garlic. Drizzle over the
carrots while still warm.

Mix in the cumin, green onion and parsley. The salad can be served warm but
it's best at room temperature when the flavors have had a chance to meld.

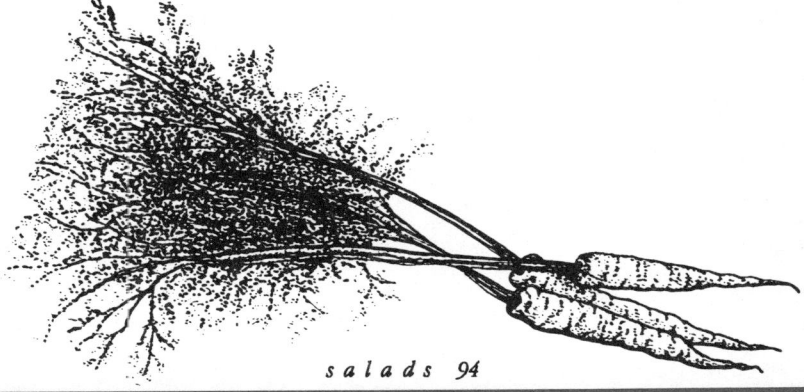

• CORN SALAD

When the main course is going to be barbecue and the event is potluck, what are you going to bring?

I gave it some thought when invited to a "pig out" in Cincinnati. The host promised succulent roast pig, prime rib and chicken.

A pig roast is no time for anything fancy and I contemplated various spicy concoctions, finally settling on a jazzed-up version of corn salad. It pairs fresh summer corn and tomatoes with lively seasonings.

It's important not to overcook the corn.

Makes 8 servings

4 ears fresh corn, husked
3 tablespoons freshly
  squeezed lime juice
2 tablespoons vegetable oil
2 small tomatoes, peeled,
  seeded and diced
1/4 cup minced onion
2 jalapeno peppers, seeds
  and ribs removed

1 large clove garlic, minced
1 teaspoon salt
freshly ground black pepper
3 tablespoons minced fresh
  cilantro or parsley
2 avocados, peeled and
  cut into chunks

Fill a large pot with water, bring to a boil. Add corn. Cover. Cook 3-5 minutes, depending on maturity of corn.

Remove corn from water. Cool. Cut off kernels into a large bowl, toss with 2 tablespoons of the lime juice and oil. Add the tomatoes and minced onion. Cut the jalapeno peppers into a fine mince; add to salad with the garlic, salt and pepper. Stir in 2 tablespoons of the cilantro. Cover and refrigerate.

Toss the avocado chunks with the remaining tablespoon of lime juice to prevent darkening. Cover and refrigerate until ready to use.

Before serving, toss the avocado and remaining tablespoon of cilantro with the salad.

NOTE: Add a can of drained and rinsed black beans for another dimension.

• THAI CUCUMBER SALAD

A sweet and sour cucumber salad is a traditional accompaniment to satays, the grilled, skewered snacks served in Thailand (see appetizers). Depending on who you talk to, it may be spiked with hot pepper, but it's not necessary.

In this country, the salad is also a good accompaniment to grilled chicken and seafood.

Makes 4 to 6 small servings

1 medium cucumber, peeled and seeded
1/2 cup vinegar
2 tablespoons sugar
1/4 teaspoon salt
1/2 cup chopped onion
1 jalapeno (preferably red), minced
2 sprigs cilantro (optional)

Cut the cucumber into quarters lengthwise and slice crosswise. Combine the vinegar, sugar and salt and stir to dissolve sugar. Add the cucumber, onion and jalapeno. Set aside until ready to serve.

Sprinkle with slivered cilantro leaves.

NOTE: A touch of sesame oil is a nice addition.

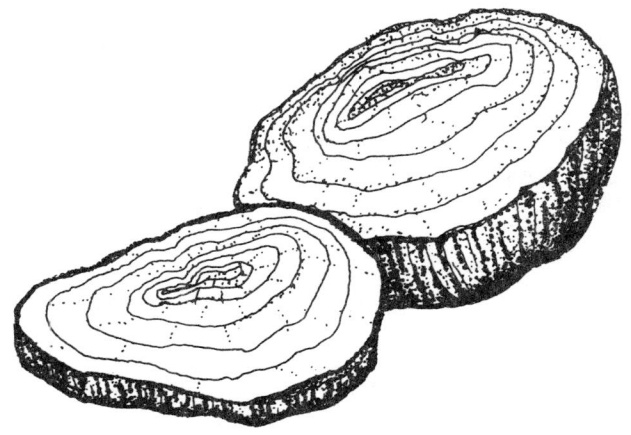

• RED, WHITE & GREEN BEAN SALAD

Summer farm markets bring wonderful crops of green beans, the likes of which never are seen the rest of the year.

This salad combines the beautiful colors of green beans and red bell peppers with the crunch of jicama, that Mexican vegetable that has a texture similar to water chestnuts.

For added flavor, sprinkle the salad with minced cilantro, or, if you prefer, basil.

Makes 4 to 6 servings

1 pound small green beans, cleaned
salt
1 red bell pepper
1/2 jicama, about 1/2 pound
2 tablespoons vinegar

1/2 teaspoon ground cumin
salt and freshly ground
 black pepper
6 tablespoons olive oil
1 lime

Bring a large pot of water to a boil and add 1/2 teaspoon salt. Add the beans, and cover only long enough to bring the water back to a boil. Cook, 3 to 5 minutes, just until the beans are tender-crisp. Drain and rinse with cold water to stop the cooking. Set aside.

Seed the pepper and cut into julienne strips the same size as the beans. Peel the jicama, removing the skin and the fibrous outer layer. Cut into julienne the size of the beans and peppers.

Blend the vinegar, cumin, 1/2 teaspoon of salt and pepper to taste. Add the oil and mix well. Pour over the pepper and jicama strips and let marinate at least a half hour.

Just before serving, toss the mixture with the green beans and sprinkle with lime juice. If tossed ahead of time, the lime juice will diminish the bean's bright green color.

• TIP

Jicama, which looks like a big brown potato, is available in many supermarket produce sections. Avoid any that look wrinkled or are soft.

• SPINACH & FRESH BASIL SALAD

A green salad has a new meaning these days. The salad may include a variety of colorful lettuces, which may or may not be green. The flavors may be as bold as spicy Italian arugula and as mild as French mache.

And the greens may share equal billing with herbs.

Small leaves of basil add an exotic flavor to salads. For added intrigue, use leaves plucked from the opal basil plant, which is worth growing if only for the purple color.

Makes 6 to 8 servings

6 cups fresh spinach leaves, washed and dried
2 cups fresh basil leaves, washed and dried
1/2 cup olive oil
3 cloves garlic, minced
1/2 cup pine nuts
1/4 pound prosciutto, julienned*
salt and freshly ground black pepper
3/4 cup freshly grated Parmesan cheese

Combine the spinach and basil in a bowl. Heat the olive oil over medium heat; add the garlic and pine nuts and saute just until the nuts begin to brown slightly. Stir in the prosciutto and cook 1 minute more. Season lightly with salt (the cheese is salty) and generously with pepper. Toss the salad with the warm dressing and cheese (You may want to use less cheese, so start with half.) Serve immediately.

NOTE: There is no vinegar or lemon juice in the salad.

*If necessary, you may substitute Canadian bacon or lean baked ham, but the flavor won't be the same.

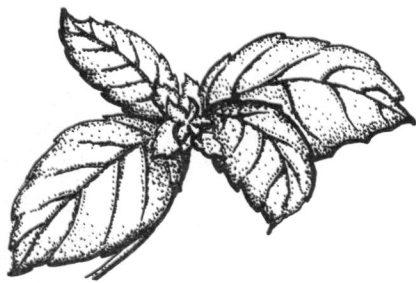

• SPINACH SALAD WITH SHERRY VINAIGRETTE

In the circus of life, sometimes the sideshow steals the applause from the main event.

It's that way at the dinner table, too. Because I'm always testing recipes, any dinner is apt to be made up of two, three or four new dishes. Often, it's not the main course that's memorable. It's the side dish, the go-with that was added to flesh out the menu.

So it was that during a shrimp extravaganza I made a simple salad with fresh, tender spinach. It was the dressing made with sherry vinegar that made the difference. That vinegar has a wonderful nutty aroma and taste, but is less expensive than nutty oils. It gives excitement to simple vinaigrette when used sparingly.

Makes 4 servings

2 tablespoons sherry vinegar
6 tablespoons light olive oil
1/4 teaspoon salt
freshly ground black pepper
1 clove garlic, halved
1 pound spinach leaves
1 tomato, peeled, seeded and chopped

Blend the vinegar, oil, salt, pepper and garlic; set aside to ripen flavors. Wash and dry the spinach leaves; tear leaves into a serving bowl. Top with tomatoes. Toss with the dressing, reserving any excess.

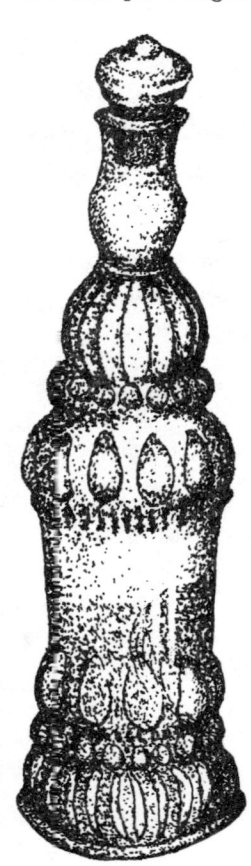

• ASIAN PEAR SALAD

Asian pears – also known as pear apples – have caught on so well with the American consumer that there are now several varieties available at the supermarket.

The smooth-skinned Asian pear comes swaddled in a little net panty. Another, brown and dull, may be mounded nearby.

The fruit is very crisp and juicy, but sweetness varies. In tasting the two, I thought the brown-skinned variety had more flavor.

They can be eaten as is, but are good in winter salads. In this one, the saltiness of the ham pairs wonderfully with the fruit.

Makes 6 servings

3 Asian pears
6 green onions,
1/4 pound ham,
    sliced 1/8-inch thick*
1 ¹/₂ tablespoons rice vinegar

1/2 teaspoon sugar
4 tablespoons vegetable oil
mixed salad greens

Peel and core the pears and slice 1/4-inch thick. If not using immediately, toss with the juice of half a lemon to prevent browning.

Trim excess top 3 inches from onions and discard. Slice onions, both white and green parts, very thin. Julienne the ham into fine shreds.

Blend the vinegar and sugar until the sugar dissolves. Add the oil and mix.

Toss the pears and most of the onions and the julienned ham with the dressing. Serve on top of mixed greens and sprinkle with remaining onions.

*Proscuitto is best, but good-quality cooked ham can be used.

• SARA'S POTATO SALAD

The potato salads of family reunions are usually the kind made with mayonnaise, although my mother always took her old-fashioned version made with a creamy, sweet and sour boiled dressing.

French-style potato salad, made with a vinaigrette dressing, is appealing, but this recipe from Sara Pearce (former food editor of the "Cincinnati Enquirer") elevates that approach to a real winner. The original recipe was from the "New York Times", but Sara tinkered with the recipe, increasing the garlic and herbs. For this recipe, the herbs must be fresh, not dried.

In theory the recipe serves six, but since it invites seconds, it may only serve four. Since it keeps well, make a double batch.

Serves 4 to 6

2 ¹/₂ pounds small red potatoes, unpeeled*

5 tablespoons olive oil

3 cloves garlic, coarsely chopped

salt and pepper

1 tablespoon red wine or sherry vinegar

1 tablespoon whole grain mustard

1 teaspoon fresh minced chives

2 teaspoons fresh minced rosemary

Wash the potatoes and pat dry. Cut in half, or, if the potatoes are medium-sized, in quarters. Toss the potatoes with 3 tablespoons of the olive oil and arrange in a single layer in a baking dish. Sprinkle with the chopped garlic and salt and pepper to taste.

Bake at 425 degrees for 30 to 40 minutes, stirring at least three times to prevent sticking. Remove from oven when potatoes are just tender.

Make a vinaigrette with the vinegar, remaining 2 tablespoons olive oil, mustard, and salt and pepper to taste. Toss with potatoes while they are still warm. Let cool to room temperature

Just before serving, sprinkle with the fresh herbs and toss to combine.

* Or use yellow Yukon Gold potatoes.

• THE TRELLIS STRAWBERRY MACADAMIA SALAD

When Marcel Desaulniers, chef-owner of The Trellis restaurant in Williamsburg, Va. was in the area for a celebrity fund-raiser, his contribution was an elegant strawberry macadamia nut salad .It doesn't take chef's skills to make the salad; it's easy to do for dinner for eight.

The salad combines the sweetness of strawberries with the richness of macadamia nuts and the tang of balsamic vinegar. It can be arranged on the plate ahead of time and dressed at the last minute.

Makes 8 servings

1 cup toasted macadamia nuts
1 pint large strawberries washed and dried
1/3 cup balsamic vinegar
1 cup vegetable oil
salt and pepper
1 large head bibb lettuce, washed and dried
4 large Belgian endives, washed and dried

Split the macadamia nuts in half and set aside. Stem strawberries and slice about 1/4-inch thick. Using a food processor, puree 2/3 cup of the sliced strawberries with the vinegar. Add the oil and process for 30 to 40 seconds until the dressing is well combined. Season with salt and pepper. If the berries are not sweet, add a teaspoon or two of sugar. The dressing can be made ahead, covered and refrigerated for up to 2 days.

Put 2 leaves of bibb lettuce on each of 8 chilled plates. Arrange 7 leaves of endive on top, like spokes in a wheel. Fan out 8 slices of strawberries in the center. If assembling ahead, cover with plastic wrap and refrigerate plates.

Just before serving, spoon 3 to 4 tablespoons dressing over the strawberries and top with the toasted nuts.

• MEXICAN TOMATO SALAD

As herbs capture the fancy of cooks, new ones catch on. Fresh cilantro is favored by many young chefs these days, though not every one likes the pungent herb.

Cilantro, also called coriander or Chinese parsley, is widely used in Mexican and Chinese dishes. It was Mexican tomato salsa that inspired me to come up with this recipe for Mexican tomato salad, which just uses the salsa ingredients in another way.

For a variation, top the tomatoes with cubes of avocado.

Makes 4 servings

4 home-grown tomatoes, peeled and sliced
salt and pepper
1 jalapeno pepper, seeded and finely minced
1 small sweet onion, chopped coarsely
1/4 cup cilantro leaves, finely minced
1 tablespoon lime juice
3 tablespoons olive oil

Arrange tomatoes on a serving platter, overlapping slightly. Sprinkle with salt and pepper. Scatter the minced pepper and onion over the tomatoes. Sprinkle cilantro leaves on top.

Blend the lime juice and olive oil with 1/4 teaspoon of salt and drizzle over the salad. The salad can marinate a while but do not refrigerate.

• CHICKEN & AVOCADO SALAD
WITH GINGER-ORANGE DRESSING

I am a purist about salad dressing. It's so easy to mix a little good olive oil and vinegar or lemon juice, that it never occurs to me to buy the bottles with the never-ending list of ingredients. Fresh is so good I don't need preservatives and stabilizers.

I do vary the dressings, sometimes with different vinegars, or a dab of Dijon mustard, or with the addition of garlic or herbs. Recently I tried a recipe that included ginger root, onion and orange in the dressing. It was wonderful.

In this salad the addition of chicken makes it an entree. Leave the chicken out and you have an attractive and unusual salad to go with your meal.

Makes 4 servings

1 tablespoon chopped onion
1/4-inch slice peeled fresh
   ginger root
1/4 cup vegetable oil
1/4 cup olive oil
2 tablespoons white wine vinegar
1/2 orange, peel and
   membranes removed

1/4 teaspoon salt
1/8 teaspoon white pepper
1 $1/_2$ pounds cooked chicken
   breasts
lettuce
1 ripe avocado, peeled and sliced
1/2 red onion, sliced and
   separated into rings

To make dressing, put onion and ginger in blender or food processor; process until finely chopped. Add oil, vinegar, orange, salt and pepper and blend.

Slice the chicken into 1/4-inch pieces and marinate in some of the dressing. Arrange lettuce on serving plates; top with chicken, avocado, onion rings and drizzle with dressing. Garnish with additional orange slices if desired.

• TIP

An easy way to cook boneless chicken breasts for salads is to sprinkle them with salt, wrap in plastic wrap and steam for 12 minutes on a steamer rack over boiling water.

CURRIED SHRIMP SALAD WITH GRAPES

*In my recipe box, this salad has the handwritten annotation of "wonderful."
And, it can be an incredibly easy summer supper – if you buy cooked
shrimp along with some grapes at the supermarket. All you have to do is toast
some nuts and combine the ingredients.*

*Tuck the salad in the refrigerator for a while, pour a glass of wine and relax.
It doesn't get any easier than this.*

Makes 4 servings

1 $1/_2$ tablespoons curry powder
1 cup mayonnaise
dash cayenne
freshly ground white pepper
3/4 cup red seedless grapes
1 $1/_4$ pounds shrimp, shelled, deveined, cooked and chilled
1/2 cup blanched almonds, slivered and toasted

Mix the curry powder, mayonnaise, cayenne and a generous sprinkling of white
pepper. Add grapes and shrimp. Refrigerate for 1 hour.

To serve, arrange on salad greens and top with slivered almonds.

• SAUCES &
CONDIMENTS

• GUILIANO'S TOMATO SAUCE

Guiliano Bugialli is one of the great cooking teachers. He is a passionate man, with flashing brown eyes, an infectious laugh and a commitment to preserving the best of Italian cuisine.

He teaches cooking in his schools in New York and Florence, but is frequently on the road giving demonstrations in cooking schools around the United States.

He preaches purism in matters as simple as tomato sauce. It is not the tomato sauce of Italian-American restaurants, so dark and thick you could stand a spoon in it. Not a sauce simmered all day long.

Rather, it is a light tomato sauce served throughout Italy. With the addition of butter and basil, it is a lovely way to sauce pasta.

Makes sauce for 8 first- course servings of pasta

3 tablespoons olive oil
1 medium clove garlic, peeled
1 pound can imported tomatoes, drained
salt and freshly ground black pepper

Heat the oil in a small saucepan over medium heat; add the garlic and saute 3 minutes. Discard garlic. Add tomatoes, cover and cook 20 minutes. Pass through a food mill, using the disk with the smallest holes to remove seeds and skin, into a saucepan. Don't use a food processor for the seeds that remain can be bitter.

Add salt—and, like most Italians, Bugialli uses salt generously—and freshly ground pepper. Let the sauce reduce over medium heat for 15 minutes.

To serve, Bugialli style, place 8 tablespoons butter in a big bowl set over the pasta pot. When pasta is cooked, drain it and toss with the softened butter. Pour the tomato sauce over and cover with 1 cup freshly grated Farmigiano Reggiano cheese and 10 large leaves basil that have been torn. Toss and serve immediately.

NOTE: Figure on 3 ounces pasta per serving.

• *TOMATO & RED BELL PEPPER SAUCE*

There are two good things about August. One is knowing, about midway through the month, that cooler weather is on the way. And, from the cooks' point of view, it's the availability of red bell peppers at the farmers' markets, at prices we can all afford.

While both peppers and homegrown tomatoes are available, indulge in this fresh-tasting sauce for pasta. For a richer sauce reduce a cup of cream by half, then whisk it into the tomato pepper sauce. It's wonderful with chicken or seafood.

Makes 2²/₃ cups

> 2 tablespoons butter
> 4 large red bell peppers, seeded and cut into 1-inch chunks
> 2³/₄ pounds tomatoes, peeled, seeded and chopped
> salt and freshly ground pepper

Melt 1 tablespoon of the butter in a heavy skillet over medium-low heat. Add the peppers and cook until tender, about 10 minutes. Transfer the peppers to a food processor and puree until smooth.

Return to the skillet, add the tomatoes and remaining butter. Cook over medium heat, stirring frequently, until the liquid evaporates and the mixture is thick. Season with salt and pepper.

The mixture is best when fresh, but it can be refrigerated for one day and reheated over low heat.

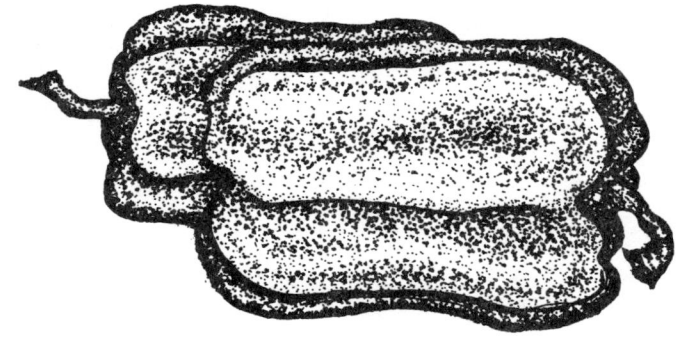

• PEASANT SAUCE

While I'm not one to use convenience foods, there are some canned foods that are essential. I'd hate to do without canned tomatoes. Even when tomatoes are in season, the canned plum tomatoes usually make a more flavorful sauce.

This recipe, from the cookbook author Sarah Leah Chase, is one of the best I've tasted. What sets this sauce apart is the large amount of onions that produce a smoky, sweet taste in the meatless sauce. It's wonderful on pasta, as a topper for baked potatoes or a super relish for hamburgers.

Makes enough sauce for 1 pound pasta

1/2 cup fruity extra virgin olive oil

3 large yellow onions, chopped medium fine

1 tablespoon salt

2 $\frac{1}{2}$ tablespoons tomato paste

1 35-ounce can plum tomatoes, undrained

Heat oil in large saucepan over high heat until sizzling hot. Add the onion and saute, stirring frequently for 5 minutes. Reduce the heat to medium and cook the onions, stirring frequently, just until they begin to turn golden brown, about 25 minutes.

Stir in the salt and tomato paste, add the canned tomatoes and simmer the sauce uncovered for 30 minutes. Toss with hot pasta or use as a topping for baked potatoes. The sauce can be also be refrigerated or frozen.

• SHIITAKE SALSA

For today's lifestyles, main courses that are simply grilled or broiled are daily winners. But they're dressed up with salsas in infinite variety.

This recipe for a shiitake mushroom salsa goes beautifully with full-flavored fish such as tuna, but it does just as well with steak. It's easy to make, though there is a bit of chopping to do.

Makes 6 to 8 servings

1 tablespoon butter
2 cups thinly sliced fresh
  shiitake mushrooms
1 tablespoon minced garlic
1/4 cup teriyaki sauce
1/2 teaspoon chili-garlic sauce*

1 tablespoon Oriental sesame oil
1/2 teaspoon black pepper
1/4 cup rice wine vinegar
1 tomato
1/2 cup sliced green onions
1 bunch cilantro

In a large skillet, melt the butter and stir fry the mushrooms and garlic over medium heat, until mushrooms are tender. Remove from heat, pour in the teriyaki sauce and return to heat, and cook, stirring for 1 to 2 minutes. Remove from heat and cool.

Combine the chili-garlic sauce, oil, pepper and vinegar and pour over the mushrooms. Cut the tomato in half and scoop out seeds. Dice the tomato and add to the mushrooms with the green onions.

Rinse and dry the cilantro in a salad spinner; discard stems. Chop the leaves. Stir half into the mushrooms. Just before serving, add the remaining cilantro.

*Jarred chili-garlic sauce is sold in Oriental food stores. The sauce is good to have on hand in the refrigerator to spice up other dishes.

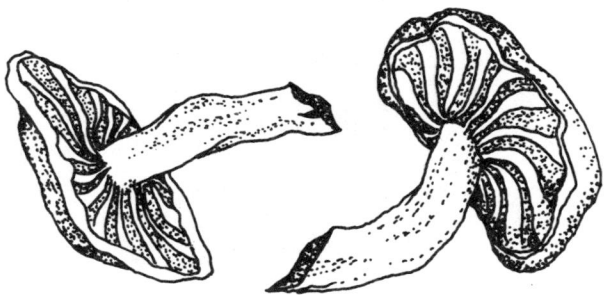

• *MANGO SALSA*

Cooks who travel on their stomachs flock to the Southwest to explore that cuisine. The restaurants there provide a varied introduction to salsas, which have quickly become so popular in this country that the jarred kind has pushed ahead of ketchup in sales. But bottled salsas rate a distant second to fresh versions.

American chefs have expanded the borders of this originally Mexican staple. A pioneer is Mark Miller of Santa Fe's Coyote Cafe and now Red Sage in Washington, D.C.

Miller's mango salsa, a combination of gold and red with flecks of green, is stunning on the plate. It's good with poultry, pork and even grilled seafood.

Remember that mango is a fruit, not a bell pepper, which is curiously called a mango in parts of the Midwest. The salsa can also be made with cantaloupe, peaches or papaya.

Makes 2 1/4 cups

2 mangoes, ripe but firm
1/2 red bell pepper, seeded
2 jalapeno peppers, finely minced
2 tablespoons minced cilantro

1 tablespoon rice wine vinegar*
juice of 1 lime
sugar to taste (optional)

Peel the mangoes and cut flesh away from the seed. Cut into slices and dice. Cut the pepper into a dice the same size.

Combine the mango, red pepper, jalapeno, cilantro, vinegar and lime juice. It is unlikely you'll need to add sugar, but taste and see.

NOTE: Be sure to buy the plain, unseasoned rice wine vinegar, not the seasoned version.

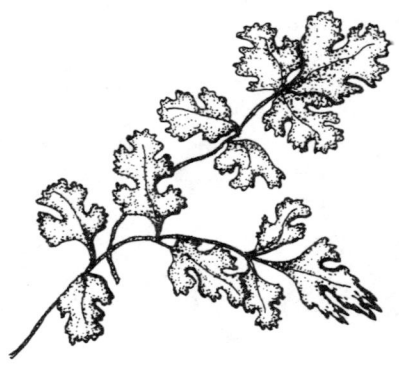

• SALSA PICO DE GALLO

In Mexico, salsa is as essential as beans. I miss both when I come back home from my usual winter vacation. So I make salsa regularly, and in summer, when the tomatoes are fresh, my favorite is one called pico de gallo.

It combines the best tomatoes with the bold flavors of hot chilies, cilantro and lime. It's good on everything, starting with Mexican grilled chicken (see index). Try it with steak, grilled tuna, even a grilled cheese sandwich.

Makes 8 servings

1 ¹/₂ white onions, chopped
4 tomatoes, about 2 pounds, peeled, seeded and chopped very fine
2 to 4 chilies serrano, finely chopped (including seeds)
1/2 cup fresh cilantro, minced
1/2 teaspoon salt
juice of 1 lime
2 tablespoons olive oil

Put all ingredients in a bowl and let marinate for at least 1 hour.
Start with one chili and add more if your taste can stand the heat
   Refrigerate leftovers.

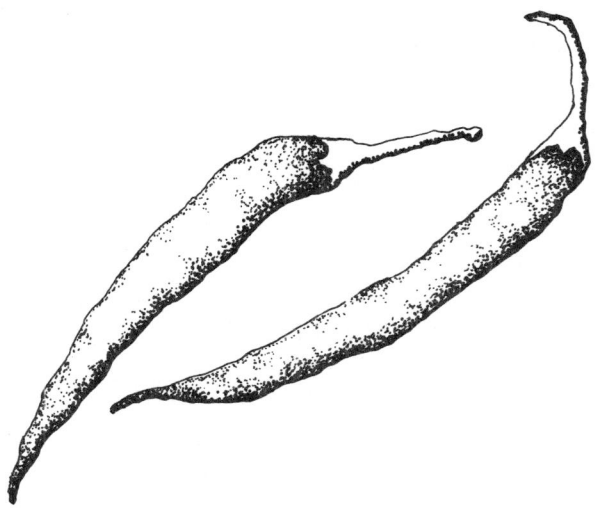

• CILANTRO PESTO

We all know what pesto is. It's that heady mixture of fresh basil and oil, garlic and pine nuts, Parmesan and butter. Right?

It's not that simple. Some cooks use Parmesan cheese; others add romano. Some add parsley to the basil, or make a colorful purple pesto from opal basil.

Actually, the word "pesto" stems from the technique of pounding a mixture to a paste. Contemporary chefs have taken liberties with the Italian classic. They've substituted hazelnuts, pistachios, almonds, and peanuts for the pine nuts. And they've made pesto of other herbs, including mint, cilantro, tarragon, even dill.

Marilyn Hampstead of Michigan's Fox Hill Farm and defender of the faith, objects — but only to the name.

"They're nice green sauces, but I draw the line at what people can call pesto," she says.

That said, here's a recipe for an East-West cilantro pesto. Make it shortly before serving; the flavors deteriorate quickly.

Makes 1 1/2 cups

4 tablespoons butter
3 tablespoons unsalted, dry-roasted peanuts
1 cup lightly packed cilantro leaves
1/2 large jalapeno pepper, seeded if desired
1/4 teaspoon salt
1/2 cup peanut or other mild vegetable oil
1/4 cup grated Parmesan cheese

Process butter and peanuts in a food processor until pureed. Add cilantro, pepper and salt and process briefly until blended. Drizzle in oil with machine running. Toss with freshly cooked pasta and sprinkle with cheese.

Garnish with chopped peanuts and sprigs of fresh cilantro if desired.

• PEANUT SAUCE

We tend to think of peanuts as American because of the work of George Washington Carver. But they're not native to this hemisphere, and are widely used in cuisines of other countries, from Africa to Asia.

In Thailand and other neighboring countries, a spicy peanut sauce is served alongside the skewered satays that are everyday street food (see appetizers). Here's one version.

Makes 2 cups

1 $^1/_2$ cups canned unsweetened coconut milk*
1 $^1/_2$ tablespoons red curry paste*
1/2 cup chunky peanut butter, preferably unsalted
1 $^1/_2$ tablespoons lime juice
1 $^1/_2$ tablespoons sugar
1 tablespoon fish sauce*

In a small saucepan, heat 3/4 cup of the coconut milk. Add the red curry paste and cook, stirring until the fat separates and droplets of oil appear on the surface.

Add the peanut butter, lime juice, sugar, fish sauce and remaining 3/4 cup coconut milk. Continue cooking—stirring to prevent scorching— for 8 to 10 minutes, until the sauce thickens slightly. Serve at room temperature.

*Available at Oriental markets. Fish sauce keeps well, as does curry paste when refrigerated.

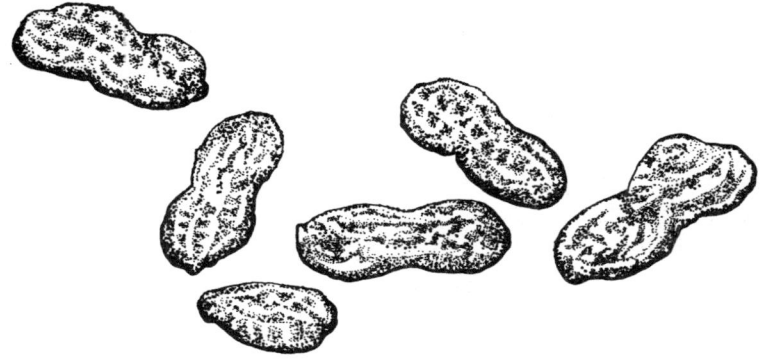

• CRANBERRY CHUTNEY

This recipe for cranberry chutney makes enough to fill eight 8-ounce jars. Make it to enjoy with Thanksgiving dinner and give away the rest as Christmas presents.

It is novel, this marriage of the taste of New England's cranberries and the Southwest's chilies. It is pungent with the pucker of wine vinegar, sweetened with brown sugar and molasses. It's good with pork as well as poultry.

The recipe is the creation of Willie Bishop, owner of the Santa Fe Bar & Grill in Berkeley, Calif.

Makes eight 8-ounce jars

3 12-ounce packages
  fresh cranberries
2 cups raisins
2 cups chopped onions
1 ¹/₂ cups chopped red
  bell peppers*
6 cloves garlic, chopped
6 small, dried, red chilies
  crumbled
3 cups red wine vinegar

1/2 cup molasses
2 cups firmly packed brown sugar
1 ¹/₂ teaspoons ground ginger
1/4 teaspoon ground cloves
1/2 teaspoon ground cinnamon
1/2 teaspoon ground allspice
1 tablespoon salt

Combine all ingredients in a heavy-bottomed stainless steel or enameled pot and simmer over low heat, uncovered for 1 ¹/₂ hours, until thick. Stir occasionally to prevent sticking. Spoon while hot into sterilized jars. Seal and cool. Refrigerate those designated for gift giving.

*Green bell peppers can be substituted in a pinch, but they lack the sweet flavor.

• MARINATED VIDALIA ONIONS

It seems a shame to use supersweet Vidalia onions as you would any onion. These onions deserve to be showcased.

Some purists love them in a simple sandwich, nothing more than a thick slice of onion on bread spread with butter or mayo. I welcome them in spring salads, after having had my fill of the sharp bite of winter onions.

This recipe for marinated onions is a good condiment to serve with hamburgers or steak. Left to marinate for 24 hours, the onions soften in the sweet-sour marinade.

Makes 16 servings

4 jumbo Vidalia onions   1/4 cup vinegar
3/4 cup sugar   1/2 teaspoon salt
3/4 cup salad oil   1/4 teaspoon coarse black pepper

Peel and slice the onions and place in a 2-quart dish that has a tight cover. Combine the sugar, oil, vinegar, salt and pepper and pour over the onions. Cover and refrigerate for at least 24 hours. They're still good after 48 hours.

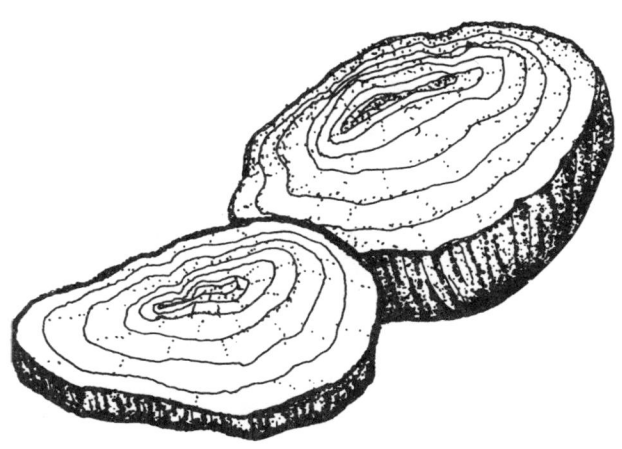

- *NOTES*

• DESSERTS

• WARM CHOCOLATE TARTS

If it's true that one great recipe makes a cookbook, then Ronald Johnson's "Company Fare" is a winner.

That's because Johnson has a recipe for a make-ahead, have-on-hand, freezer-to-oven, triple-chocolate dessert that's sinfully rich and positively sensuous.

He calls the recipe, attributed to the defunct restaurant Rakal in New York, "a chocolate tart" but it really isn't. Baked in individual dishes, it is cakelike at the edges with a warm, puddinglike chocolate center. Served warm with vanilla ice cream it's a double treat.

Just pop these tarts in the oven as you clear the table and serve dessert nonchalantly, as if you did this all the time.

Makes 6 servings

4 ounces bittersweet
  or semisweet chocolate
1 1/2 ounces unsweetened
  chocolate
10 tablespoons unsalted butter

1/2 cup plus 2 tablespoons sugar
1/2 cup plus 2 teaspoons flour
1 1/2 tablespoons unsweetened cocoa
3/4 teaspoon baking powder
3 large eggs

Lightly butter six 1-cup souffle dishes or oven-proof custard cups. Melt both chocolates with butter in the top of a double boiler set over simmering water. Add sugar and stir until it dissolves. Scrape into the bowl of a mixer. Add flour, cocoa, baking powder and eggs. Beat with an electric mixer for 7 to 8 minutes until it thickens to a mousselike consistency. Divide among the dishes, cover with foil and freeze at least 3 hours.

Preheat oven to 375 degrees. Remove foil and bake the tarts 11 to 13 minutes. Watch closely at end of baking time. First edges set, then the center shows moist and shiny, then just a minute after that they are cooked. DON'T overbake. Cool 10 minutes, then invert onto dessert plates.

NOTE: The desserts do not rise.

• APPLE WALNUT TORTE

I grew up in a family where the gathering of black walnuts and hickory nuts was a ritual of fall. We always went to fields near Fort Ancient about the time the leaves began to turn.

Dad hulled the walnuts and throughout the winter would sit by the fire and crack a big bowlful, picking out the nutmeats.

Because my interest in the kitchen started with cookie baking, I developed the taste for flavorful black walnuts in desserts.

I use black walnuts in any cookie recipe that calls for pecans or English walnuts, but am especially tempted by a recipe that specifies black walnuts. Here's one from the booklet put together by the women of the First Church of God in Camden, where they have an annual black walnut festival. It is deceptively simple to make, and very good.

Makes 6 to 8 servings

1 egg, beaten lightly	1/2 cup flour
3/4 cup sugar	pinch of salt
1 cup sliced apples	1/4 teaspoon vanilla
1 teaspoon baking powder	1/4 cup chopped black walnuts

Combine the beaten egg with the sugar and apples. Stir in the remaining ingredients and pour into a 9-inch greased pie tin.

Bake at 350 degrees for 25 minutes. Serve warm or cold, with whipped cream or ice cream.

• MACADAMIA NUT TART

Macadamia nuts, like pine nuts, are a luxury but there is no good substitute for either. Because this recipe uses three-fourths of a pound of nuts, it's definitely one to be saved for special occasions.

The tart has a cookie-like crust and is very rich and sweet. It's smart to cut it into modest portions.

The recipe is shared by Kitty Sachs, proprietor of Kitty's Restaurant, where it's sometimes served.

Makes 12 servings

Crust:	Filling:
1/2 cup butter	1 cup brown sugar
1/2 cup sugar	1/3 cup butter
2 egg yolks	2 tablespoons plus 1 teaspoon maple syrup
1 teaspoon vanilla	2 tablespoons plus 1 teaspoon light corn syrup
1 1/2 cups flour	3 tablespoons cream
	3/4 pound macadamia nuts*

By hand or with a food processor, cream the butter and sugar; beat in the yolks one at a time. Add vanilla and flour; mix until dough forms a ball. If the dough is sticky, refrigerate for 20 minutes. Press dough to 1/2-inch thickness in a 9-inch tart pan. Chill for 30 minutes.

Preheat oven to 350 degrees. Cover dough with foil, fill with pie weights, rice or beans; bake for 15 minutes, uncover and bake 5 minutes longer. Cool.

Bring butter, sugar, syrups and cream to a boil in a heavy-bottomed saucepan. Boil 1 minute. Place nuts in the cooled crust and pour the hot filling over. Bake at 350 degrees for 5 minutes, until filling bubbles. Cool for 2 hours on a rack before cutting.

* The recipe calls for unsalted nuts but salted roasted nuts worked fine.

• FRESH LEMON PUDDING

A friend of mine, a New England cooking teacher, calls this lemon pudding "absolute manna from heaven." The British would call it lemon curd, which is one of the uglier words in the English language, so I stick with pudding.

It is fragrant with fresh lemon, and though sweet, it's tart enough to wake up the taste buds of people who are used to boxed pudding mixes.

It can be used as a pudding or dessert spread. For an easy dessert, pile the cooked pudding into a phyllo crust and top with whipped cream.

In this recipe, don't use bottled lemon juice. It must be freshly squeezed juice.

If served as pudding the recipe will serve four. The recipe makes enough for one pie.

Makes 2 $\frac{1}{2}$ cups

3 lemons	3 whole eggs
1 stick butter	3 egg yolks
1/4 teaspoon salt	1/2 cup whipping cream (optional)
1 $\frac{1}{2}$ cups sugar	

Juice the three lemons and grate the rind of one of them. Melt the butter in the top of a double boiler, set over simmering water. Add the lemon rind and strained juice, the salt and sugar and mix well with a spoon.

Beat the whole eggs and yolks together with a hand beater. Add to the lemon-sugar mixture and cook over the simmering (not boiling) water, stirring from time to time. After about 10 minutes, the mixture will begin to bubble. Stir or whisk constantly until the pudding is thick and shiny — the white froth will disappear.

Cool the pudding. It can be served as is, or whip the cream and stir it into the cooled pudding to lighten it.

• BLUEBERRY CRUMBLE

As a matter of principle, I think desserts – at least those that are rich and sweet with sugar – should be reserved for special occasions. And what's more special than the beginning of blueberry season?

How I love those berries. When I was a girl it was a rare treat to eat bowls of berries with real, heavy cream and spoonfuls of sugar.

These days I'll make a cool meal on a hot summer day by filling half a cantaloupe with lightly sweetened blueberries. But my favorite blueberry dish is a sinfully easy dessert called blueberry crumble.

It's similar to other fruit crumbles, except with blueberries, all you have to do is wash the fruit – no peeling, pitting, coring or slicing.

Makes 4-6 servings

3 cups blueberries	3/4 cup flour
6 tablespoons sugar	1/3 cup butter
juice of 1 lemon	6 tablespoons sugar
1/4 teaspoon cinnamon	1/2 teaspoon salt

Wash the berries and put in a buttered, 9-inch square baking dish, or casserole of a similar size. Add the sugar, lemon juice and cinnamon and stir to coat the berries.

Combine the flour, butter, sugar and salt and mix with a fork or your fingertips until the mixture is crumbly. Sprinkle the mixture over the berries and bake at 350 degrees for 30 to 40 minutes.

It's superb as is, but you can splurge and add ice cream, too.

• PHYLLO CRUST

When company is coming and you're short on time, this phyllo crust is an alternative that will earn applause.

The instructions may look complicated, but it's really quite easy if you remember to thaw the phyllo – the thin sheets of pastry that Greek cooks use to make baklava. The pie shell requires less skill than making pie crust and is better than store bought. Use it in recipes that call for a fully baked pie crust. Just don't add the filling more than 1 hour before serving.

Makes 6 to 8 servings

4 to 6 tablespoons butter, melted
6 sheets phyllo dough (about 16 by 12 inches)

The night before, place frozen phyllo dough in the refrigerator to thaw. In the morning, place package on the counter for 2 hours to finish thawing. Remove 6 sheets and re-wrap and refreeze the rest.

Brush a 9-inch pie plate with melted butter. Unfold phyllo dough and trim to squares of the proper size (you may have to cut off an inch or two). Brush one sheet of phyllo with butter and gently place it in the pie plate, allowing ends to extend over the sides. Repeat with the remaining five sheets of dough, brushing each with melted butter, and crisscrossing the layers. Gently lift the phyllo and press down so the layers of phyllo conform to the sides of the pan. Use your hands to crumple the excess dough to form a rough edge. Brush lightly with butter.

Bake in a pre-heated 350 degree oven for 15 minutes until brown and crisp. Cool on a rack.

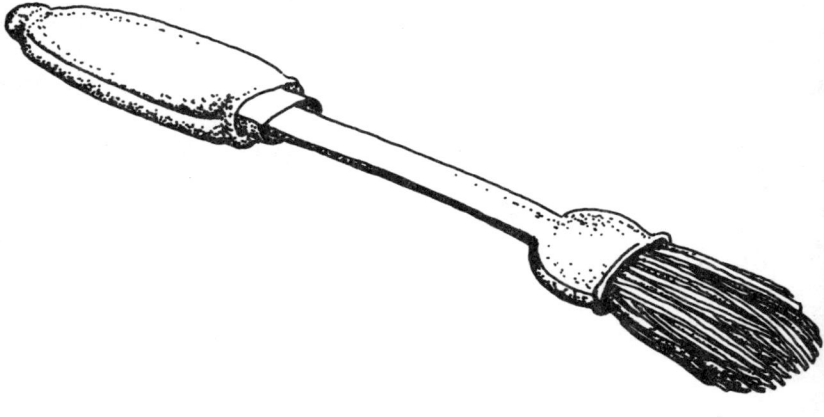

• FOOD PROCESSOR PIE CRUST

When I make pie crust I use a food processor to save time. My favorite recipe uses both vegetable shortening and cold butter, which adds to the flavor.

It's essential to have the fats chilled. Care must be taken not to over-process the dough or it will be tough. Expect the dough to have visible flakes of fat that are not blended.

This recipe makes enough for a double pie crust or two pies. If making open pies, you can make one now and freeze half the dough, well wrapped, for up to a month. Thaw and roll out when needed.

Makes crust for two 8- to 9-inch pies

2 cups all-purpose flour

1 teaspoon salt

1/2 cup vegetable
   shortening, chilled

4 tablespoons butter, chilled

6 tablespoons ice water

Insert metal blade in work bowl. Add flour, salt and fat. Process with short bursts until the mixture has the consistency of coarse meal. Stop the machine. Pour the ice water through the feed tube and process. Stop as soon as the dough begins to form a rough, moist mass. If necessary, add a bit more water. Remove from the work bowl, separate into two rounds and flatten them slightly. Wrap in waxed paper. Refrigerate 4 hours or longer (or place in the freezer for 1 hour) before rolling out.

On a lightly floured cutting board, roll out dough to 1/8-inch thickness, allowing for a 1-inch margin around the pan. Fit into pie pan gently; do not stretch or pull dough. Turn dough under to build up rim. Crimp with the tines of a fork or flute edges. Refrigerate the shell, at least 1/2 hour, until ready to use.

• TIP

To help eliminate sogginess, brush the bottom of the crust with egg white before baking. Prick the crust well to eliminate bubbling.

• PUMPKIN PRALINE PIE

When my mother made the holiday pumpkin pies, she truly made them from scratch – starting with the pie pumpkins my dad raised.

Now the pie-making job is mine and I use canned puree. This recipe has become my favorite. Because pies often must be baked ahead for holidays, the bottom crust may become soggy. Pre-baking the crust with a nutty praline glaze spread on the bottom eliminates the problem.

Because I love the taste of American black walnuts, particularly with pumpkin, I use a half-and-half mixture of black walnuts and English walnuts for the praline glaze.

Makes 8 servings

3 tablespoons butter, softened
1/3 cup brown sugar
1/3 cup walnuts
1 unbaked, 9-inch pie shell, chilled
3 eggs
1 1/2 cups pumpkin*
1/4 cup sugar

1/2 cup brown sugar
1/2 teaspoon vanilla
1/2 teaspoon salt
1 teaspoon cinnamon
1/2 teaspoon freshly ground nutmeg
1/4 teaspoon cloves
1 1/2 cups coffee cream

Preheat oven to 450 degrees. Blend the butter, 1/3 cup brown sugar and nuts. Drop onto the pie crust and spread to cover the bottom roughly. Bake the crust for 10 minutes, then set aside to cool completely.

Beat eggs slightly, add pumpkin, sugars, vanilla, salt and spices. Stir in the cream. Pour into the cooled pie shell; wrap a foil collar around the edges to protect from over-browning. Bake on the lowest shelf in a 450-degree oven for 10 minutes. Lower heat to 350 degrees and bake about 50 minutes, until filling is firm in the center and a knife inserted comes out clean.

*Use canned pumpkin puree, not pumpkin pie filling.

• RHUBARB CUSTARD PIE

This recipe for an old-time rhubarb pie was sent to me by Judith Smith of Urbana who says the recipe came from her grandmother.

The filling includes eggs, which is why it's called a rhubarb custard pie. It does not include milk.

It's so simple, I made it one morning before I came to work. And my co-workers will vouch that it's excellent.

Smith says a tender, flaky lard crust is best, but I usually use a combination of butter and vegetable shortening in my crust (see index for recipe).

She also specifies freshly grated nutmeg. That makes all the difference, as good cooks know.

Makes one 9-inch pie

pastry for a double-crust pie	generous 1/4 - 1/2 teaspoon
1 $^3/_4$ cups white sugar	freshly grated nutmeg *
dash salt	2 eggs, beaten
1/4 cup flour	4 cups diced rhubarb

In a large mixing bowl, combine the sugar, salt, flour, nutmeg and eggs. Fold in the rhubarb, stirring to coat pieces well with the egg mixture. Pour the rhubarb into chilled pie shell, piling it high. Cover with the top crust and crimp edges with a fork. Cut steam vents in the top crust.

Bake on the lower shelf of a preheated 425-degree oven for 50 minutes, until the crust is brown and the juices are bubbling. If the edges begin to overbrown, cover them with a strip of foil.

* Judy Smith uses up to 1 teaspoon ground nutmeg.

• TIP

Nutmeg, like most ground spices, has a shelf life limited to about six months. But whole nutmegs last years. Buy a little grater and a box of whole nutmegs and you'll always have fresh spice.

• *BUTTERMILK PIE*

This is the era of fancy chocolate desserts, but I'm always drawn to homey desserts such as Ohio sugar cream pie or this old-fashioned classic called buttermilk pie.

I used to hate the thought of buttermilk – because of the way it looks in the glass when someone drinks it – but it's a wonderful ingredient in everything from salad dressings to baked goods.

Makes 8 servings

1 unbaked, chilled 9-inch
  pie shell
3 large eggs
1 cup granulated sugar

2 cups buttermilk
1 tablespoon fresh lemon juice
1 teaspoon vanilla extract

Preheat oven to 450 degrees. Put a square of waxed paper inside the pie shell and fill with raw beans, rice or pie weights. Bake 10 to 12 minutes, until the dough looks set. Remove beans and waxed paper, prick the dough with a fork, then continue baking for 10 minutes longer.

Reduce oven temperature to 350 degrees. In large bowl beat the eggs, beat in the sugar, then add buttermilk, lemon juice and vanilla and mix well. Pour into baked shell. Bake 50 to 60 minutes until a knife inserted in the center comes out clean. The filling should be firm (but it will still jiggle when moved).

Let cool before serving. It can be served slightly chilled, with whipped cream but it's not necessary.

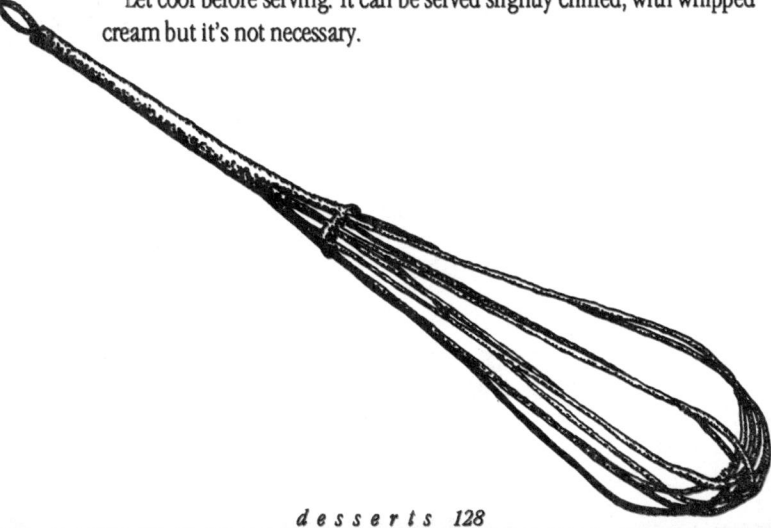

• MINCEMEAT NUT PIE

My mother, the pumpkin-pie-baker, actually didn't like pumpkin pie. She liked mincemeat pies. Children rarely do, so she didn't fix it at holidays.

When I took over the baking I made mincemeat pie for her. The best version used real mincemeat purchased at a church fair, and that's worth looking for.

Here is a mincemeat pie for people who don't like mincemeat — as well as for those who do. Adding apples to the mincemeat lightens the taste, and nuts add a little texture.

Makes 8 servings

pastry for double-crust pie, chilled
2 cups mincemeat
1 $\frac{1}{2}$ cups finely diced peeled apple
1/2 cup walnuts
1 tablespoon sugar
1 beaten egg

Preheat oven to 450 degrees. Divide pastry in half and roll out into 12-inch circles. Fit one pastry round in a 9-inch pie plate, trim 1 inch from rim of plate. Combine mincemeat, apples and nuts. Brush bottom crust with some of the beaten egg to prevent sogginess. Spoon the mincemeat mixture into the pie shell. Top with the remaining pastry round; trim and crimp edges. Brush with remaining egg. Cut vent holes in top crust to allow steam to escape.

Bake for 30-40 minutes, until the crust is evenly browned. Cool before serving. Cover edge with foil, if it begins to brown too much.

• CRANBERRY-APPLE PIE

One of my bosses wryly observes that the burden of food editors is to find a new use for cranberries each Christmas season. One year my contribution was this wonderful Shaker cranberry-apple pie.

The recipe, shared by the American Harvest restaurant in New York, comes from the Shaker community.

The cranberries provide a rosy tint and tartness. The original recipe calls for maple sugar, but a mixture of granulated sugar and maple syrup can be used.

For best results use real maple syrup and homemade pie crust. To make life simpler on the holiday, make and shape the pie crust ahead of time, folding the top crust in quarters. Refrigerate until ready to use.

Makes 6 to 8 servings

pastry for double-crust pie	1 cup sugar
3 to 4 tart apples, peeled cored and sliced	2 tablespoons maple syrup
1 ½ cups cranberries	1 tablespoon tapioca*
	3 tablespoons butter

Roll out chilled dough and place the bottom crust in a 9-inch pie tin. Pile apples high in the pan. Mash the cranberries a bit, and mix them with sugar, syrup and tapioca to draw a little juice. Pile the cranberries over the apples and dot with butter.

Moisten edge of lower crust so it will seal. Put top crust over pie, and press to bond to lower crust. Flute the edges and trim off excess dough. Cut a V in the top crust to let out steam. Brush the crust with melted butter and sprinkle with sugar to assure a nice brown crust.

Bake in a preheated 450-degree oven for 10 minutes; reduce heat to 375 degrees and bake another 30 minutes.

*The tapioca is optional, but without it, the pie will be very juicy.

• PEACHES & CREAM PIE

Friends know I rarely volunteer to bring desserts to picnics and potluck dinners. That's not where my talents lie.

I'm content to just dip sun-ripened strawberries in brown sugar and sour cream, or, in midsummer, eat cantaloupe with nothing more than a sprinkle of blueberries. But when fresh peaches are in season I'm tempted to paint the lily and add to the natural glory of the fruit.

I took this pie to a neighborhood picnic.

It is about the easiest pie you can make. All you have to do is peel and slice the peaches. Of course you can use defrosted frozen peaches as well, but why not use fresh peaches when they're available in the market?

Makes 6 to 8 servings

3/4 cup sugar
1/2 cup all purpose flour
1 unbaked 9-inch pie shell

2 cups peeled, sliced fresh peaches
1/2 teaspoon almond extract
1 cup whipping cream

Preheat the oven to 350 degrees. Blend the sugar and flour and sprinkle about a third of the mixture in the bottom of the unbaked pie shell. Smooth evenly across the pie shell. Toss the peaches with the almond extract. Add the peaches to the pie shell, keeping the slices level rather than heaping them in the pie. Sprinkle with the remaining sugar and flour mixture. Pour the cream over the top. Use a fork to move the peach slices around so they are immersed in the cream.

Bake the pie for 45 minutes. The creamy filling should be firm and lightly browned in spots on top. Cool on rack before serving.

• HOW TO DO IT

• HOW TO DO IT

Here are some tips that will make fixing these recipes – and life in the kitchen – a little more simple.

• BROWN SUGAR

If your brown sugar has turned rock-hard, place it in a bowl and microwave for 30 seconds on high. It may need another 30 seconds to soften. Or, heat the sugar in a 250-degree oven for a minute or two. Watch that it doesn't melt. As a preventive measure, tuck a piece of bread inside when you open a fresh box of brown sugar. The bread will get hard and the sugar will stay soft.

• CHICKEN BROTH

If I don't have homemade stock on hand I use reduced-salt chicken broth, because it tastes more like chicken than the salty varieties. But no one wants to open a can to use just 2 tablespoons, so do what I do: Refrigerate and skim off the fat, then pour into an ice cube tray and freeze. Bag the ready-to-use cubes of broth in a plastic freezer bag. One cube equals 2 tablespoons.

• CHILIES

Chilies, also called chili peppers and chiles, are as hot as habaneros and as mild as anaheims, with familiar jalapeno and serrano chilies in between. To tame a chili, remove both the seeds and ribs, which is where the heat is. You'll have chili flavor without heat.

• CILANTRO

Cilantro, like its parsley look-alike, is sold by the bunch. To store it, put the bunch in a glass with cold water, cover loosely with a plastic bag and refrigerate, changing the water every two days. Parsley is also best stored this way, rather than in the hydrator.

• CRANBERRIES

Fresh cranberries are available only from October through December, but you can have berries year-round if you remember to buy extra and freeze them. Just put a bag in a sealable freezer bag and they're ready to use in baking and sauces whenever you want them.

• GINGER ROOT

Fresh ginger root, available in the produce section of most supermarkets, adds a measure of heat as well as flavor. The brown skin may be peeled to make it visually more appealing, but in many dishes that's not necessary. It can be stored for a week, unwrapped, on the counter. If refrigerating, wrap loosely in paper towels and store in the hydrator. Do not seal in plastic bags, or it will tend to mold.

To use, it can be cut into slices and minced by hand or grated on a special ginger grater or pressed through a garlic press.

• LEMONS

The zest of lemons or other citrus is best removed by a zester, a special gadget that strips off the flavorful outer layer, leaving the bitter pith behind.

When grating lemons, pick rough-skinned fruit rather than smooth. Work the lemon diagonally across the grater, rather than up and down. Remember to wash the fruit before grating to remove sprays.

• MUSHROOMS

Fresh mushrooms should be stored in a paper bag — never in a plastic bag — in the vegetable hydrator. When sealed in plastic they become slimy quickly. To use, wipe clean with a damp paper towel; do not soak in water.

• NUTS & SEEDS

Both nuts and seeds are best purchased at a specialty nut store to ensure freshness. They can become rancid quickly if left on the pantry shelf, so store them in the refrigerator, or even the freezer if they will be used infrequently.

To toast nuts, place in a small, heavy, ungreased skillet and toast in the middle of a preheated 400-degree oven for 8 to 10 minutes until golden. Cool before using. When toasting sesame seeds, stir them once for even browning. Check pine nuts after 5 minutes.

• PASTA

Pasta cooked in unsalted water is virtually tasteless, so salt the water generously. How much water and how much salt? The Italian formula is to use four quarts water for each pound of pasta. Add 1 $\frac{1}{2}$ tablespoons salt to the boiling water before adding the pasta.

And no matter what you have read elsewhere, don't add oil to the water except when cooking filled pasta such as ravioli. If you use oil, the pasta will not be able to absorb the sauce. Instead, just stir the pasta well when you add it to the boiling water. Cover tightly until the water returns to a boil. Drain but do not rinse pasta.

• PEPPERS

To roast and preserve red bell peppers, broil whole peppers, turning to char all sides. Place the peppers in a brown paper bag, fold the top over and let them steam for 15 minutes. Peel the peppers over a bowl to catch the good juices. Remove seeds and ribs and slice peppers into strips. Pack with oil and some of the juices. These freeze well. They will also keep in the refrigerator, covered with oil, for a week or two.

While you're putting up peppers, plan ahead for winter when the price of red bell peppers skyrockets. Buy a bag from local farm markets in August or September when they're cheap. Just wash and dry the peppers, remove ribs and seeds and cut into cubes and slices. Freeze in a single layer on a cookie sheet, then store in sealable freezer bags. Use in any recipe in which they're cooked.

• WHIPPED CREAM

If you're whipping cream for desserts, try to buy plain pasteurized whipping cream, not the ultra-pasteurized cream that tastes "cooked" and doesn't whip as well. Whatever you buy, use a deep, narrow bowl and chill the beaters and bowl. Add confectioner's sugar and vanilla to taste.

Whipped cream can be whipped ahead, but just whip softly and refrigerate. When ready to serve, finish whipping with sugar.

• CREDITS

The following recipes were printed with permission from the publishers:

Baked Tomato Sauce with Pasta from *Classic Sicilian Cooking* by Mimmetta Lo Monte (Simon & Schuster). Copyright 1990.

Bourbon Pecans from *The Frog Commissary Cookbook* by Steve Poses and Rebecca Roller. Copyright 1985, The Commissary, Inc. By permission of Doubleday.

Butterflies and Beans from *Garden Fresh Cooking* by Judith Benn Hurley (Rodale Press). Copyright 1987.

Buttermilk Pie from *The Cafe des Artiste Cookbook* by George Lang (Clarkson Potter). Copyright 1984.

Carrots with Cranberries from *The Victory Garden Cookbook* by Marian Morash (Knopf). Copyright 1982.

Chicken in Many Mustards from the *Grill Book* by Kelly McCune (Harper & Row). Copyright 1986.

Chesapeake Bay Shrimp from *Shrimp* by Jay Harlow (Chronicle). Copyright 1989.

Cilantro Pesto from *Cooking from the Garden* by Rosalind Creasy (Sierra Club). Copyright 1988.

Ginger Pork from *The Poetical Pursuit of Food* by Sonoko Kondo (Clarkson Potter). Copyright 1986.

Lemon Roast Chicken from *More Classic Italian Cooking* by Marcella Hazan (Knopf). Copyright 1978.

Lomo de Cerdo Adobado (Spanish Pork Loin) from *Food & Wines of Spain* by Penelope Casas (Knopf). Copyright 1979.

Mango Salsa from the *Coyote Cafe Cookbook* by Mark Miller (Ten Speed Press). Copyright 1989.

Pesto Cheese Torta from *Entertaining for All Seasons* (Sunset Publishing). Copyright 1984.

Peaches and Cream Pie from *New Southern Cooking* by Natalie Dupree (Knopf). Copyright 1986.

Peasant Sauce from the *Nantucket Open House Cookbook* by Sarah Leah Chase (Workman). Copyright 1987.

Red Bell Pepper Saute from *New Almond Cookery* by Michelle Schmidt (Simon & Schuster). Copyright 1984.

Rigatoni with Roasted Red Peppers from *365 Ways to Cook Pasta* by Marie Simmons, (Harper & Row). Copyright 1988.

Roast Beef with Onion Sauce from *The Heritage of French Cooking* by the Scotto Sisters and Annie Hubert Bare (Random House). Copyright 1991.

Spinach and Fresh Basil Salad from *The Silver Palate Good Times Cookbook* by Julee Rosso and Sheila Lukens (Workman). Copyright 1984, 1985.

Warm Chocolate Tarts from *Company Fare* by Ronald Johnson (Simon & Schuster). Copyright 1991.

Wild Rice Pancakes from *The Great Chefs of Virginia*, (Donning). Copyright 1987.

• • • • • • • • •

• INDEX

142

• *NOTES*

• *NOTES*